COLLECTED WORKS OF A. ... .

SELECTED POEMS

Throughout his career, A.M. Klein struggled to define for himself the role of
the poet in the contemporary world. Deeply rooted in the traditions of Juda-
ism, and at the same time powerfully attracted by the freedom and scope of
international modernism, he sought to reconcile past and present, community
and creative individuality. Whether or not he finally achieved his own high
aims, it was, in his own words, 'something merely to entertain them.' The
result was a body of work immensely rich and varied in tone, language, and
cultural resonance.

This collection of eighty-four poems offers a representative sampling of
Klein's finest poetry, while taking into account the changing critical discourse
of the last fifty years. Anyone interested in experiencing the full range of
Klein's poetic achievement, or in understanding the complex nature of the
poet, need look no further than this eminently readable volume.

ZAILIG POLLOCK is Professor in the Department of English at Trent University.
SEYMOUR MAYNE is Professor in the Department of English at the University of
    Ottawa.
USHER CAPLAN is an editor at the National Gallery of Canada.

A.M. KLEIN

Selected Poems

EDITED BY
ZAILIG POLLOCK, SEYMOUR MAYNE,
AND USHER CAPLAN

UNIVERSITY OF TORONTO PRESS
Toronto Buffalo London

© University of Toronto Press 1997
Toronto Buffalo London
Printed in Canada

ISBN 0-8020-0734-1 (cloth)
ISBN 0-8020-7753-6 (paper)

Printed on acid-free paper

Canadian Cataloguing in Publication Data

Klein, A.M. (Abraham Moses), 1909–1972
Selected poems

(Collected works of A.M. Klein)
Includes bibliographical references and index.
ISBN 0-8020-0734-1 (bound)   ISBN 0-8020-7753-6 (pbk.)

I. Caplan, Usher, 1947–   . II. Mayne, Seymour, 1944–   .
III. Pollock, Zailig.   IV. Title.   V. Series:
Klein, A.M. (Abraham Moses), 1909–1972.   Collected works
of A.M. Klein.

PS8521.L45A6 1997   C811'.52   C97-930107-6
PR9199.3.K48A6 1997

University of Toronto Press acknowledges the financial assistance to
its publishing program of the Canada Council and the Ontario Arts
Council.

Contents

POEMS

TRANSLATIONS OF BIALIK

Acknowledgments

We would like to thank our fellow members of the A.M. Klein Research and Publication Committee for the invaluable help they offered us, both in establishing general principles for the *Selected Poems* and in arriving at a final list of poems to be included: Professor Mark Finkel-stein, Professor Noreen Golfman, Colman Klein, Sandor Klein, Professor Elizabeth Popham, Professor Linda Rozmovits, Professor M.W. Steinberg, and Dr Robert Taylor. We would also like to acknowledge the advice which we received at various stages of this project from members of the Editorial Board of the Klein Committee: Professors W.J. Keith, Robert Melançon, William H. New, Malcolm Ross, and Miriam Waddington. Unfortunately, three members of this Board did not live to see the publication of this volume: Professor Henry Kreisel, Professor T.A. Marshall, and Professor J.M. Robson.

Editors' Introduction

Throughout his career Klein entertained high, perhaps impossibly high, ambitions for his poetry. Poetry was not true poetry unless it engaged some great theme; and Klein's career as a poet is largely the record of a continuous inner struggle, through periods of silence as well as ones of intense productivity, to define and redefine such a theme, and to develop the means – emotional, intellectual, and artistic – to do it justice. It is a struggle which culminates in the great achievements of his maturity, and, then, in the bleak silence of his final years.

The essence of Klein's theme is community, more specifically, the relationship of the creative individual to the community in which he is rooted. As 'Portrait of the Poet as Landscape' tells us, the poet who cannot 'unroll our culture from his scroll' is a crippled poet. All other ambitions are, in comparison, 'mean.' For Klein, the poet's sense of self is essentially social; his primary relationship is not with God, or with a beloved, or even with his art, but with a community.

Klein first began to discover his theme and his voice as a poet in the late twenties. It is in the poetry of this period that we see the beginnings of two developments that were to prove central to Klein's sense of himself and of his art throughout his career. The first is his discovery of modernism; the second is his decision to take up Jewish themes.

Klein's discovery of modernism owed much to the group of young writers associated with the *McGill Fortnightly Review,* A.J.M. Smith, F.R. Scott, Leo Kennedy, and Leon Edel. His lifelong interest in Eliot, Yeats, Pound, and, especially, Joyce dates from this period, and his encounter with the McGill Group helped him to move beyond the somewhat self-indulgent imitations of Romantic and Victorian models that had dominated his earlier work. Stylistically, a number of poems of this period, such as 'Diary of Abraham Segal, Poet,' show the influence of modernism but, on the whole, the influence, at this stage of Klein's career, is relatively superficial. In the bulk of the poems of the period – the poems on Jewish themes – there seems to be, at least initially, a reaction against modernism, both in their use of traditional forms and in their celebration of traditional community values.

Klein's turning to Jewish themes in the late twenties opened a floodgate of inspiration for him, and, within a very short time, he began to produce some of his most accomplished poems, such as 'Portraits of a Minyan,' 'Design for Mediaeval Tapestry,' and 'Scribe.' His stance towards community at this time is, in general, celebratory rather than critical, and a number of the poems seem sentimental and quaint, no doubt a reflection of the fact that the way of life Klein was celebrating was to a large extent an antiquarian reconstruction of something which had ceased to exist in North America, and even in eastern Europe was passing out of existence. Certainly the contemporary world which Klein knew at first hand impinges little, if at all, on most of these poems. But the best works of this period show Klein engaging in a successful and moving act of imaginative re-creation, nowhere more impressively than in his poem on Spinoza, 'Out of the Pulver and the Polished Lens.'

First published in 1931, when Klein was only twenty-two, 'Out of the Pulver and the Polished Lens' is Klein's richest and most fully achieved statement of the Jewish themes which had dominated his poetry over the previous several years. In addition to Jewish themes, the poem raises broader issues concerning the ambivalent status of the poet in the modern age, issues that were to concern Klein more and more over the years as he increasingly came to see himself as a modernist. If we take 'Out of the Pulver' as a kind of credo on the part of the young Klein, it tells us that he sees his role as attempting to heal and to give purpose to a community that desperately needs his leadership. But, at the same time, the poem suggests that Klein is already beginning to see himself as something of an outcast, spurned by the community he wishes to serve. The tone of 'Out of the Pulver' is still essentially optimistic, but, even at this early stage of his career, Klein is pointing to problems that will never cease to engage him, as both a Jew and a modernist, and which he will never fully resolve.

It was probably not long after completing 'Out of the Pulver' that Klein found himself unable to continue writing in this vein which had proven artistically so rewarding. His virtual abandonment, in about 1931, of the kind of poetry he had been writing during the previous three or four years may reflect his disappointment in a lack of public recognition, as evidenced in his inability to get his poems published in book form. In any case, most of the poems which he wrote over the next couple of years are primarily intended for children. Many of the poems of this period, such as 'Bestiary,' 'Rev Owl,' and 'The Venerable Bee,' are witty and charming, and at least one, 'Heirloom,' is among the most moving Klein ever wrote. But none of them rivals in ambition such poems as 'Out of the Pulver and the Polished Lens' or 'Design for Mediaeval Tapestry.' Klein's poetry for children seems to mark a retreat from the heroic, visionary role which he had celebrated in 'Out of the Pulver and the Polished Lens,' but which he was now finding increasingly difficult to maintain.

As far as can be determined, Klein wrote no original poetry at all for several years after completing his series of children's poems. Instead, he turned to translations from Yiddish, primarily of folk songs, and from Hebrew, primarily of the modern Hebrew poet Chaim Nachman Bialik, who, like Klein, was deeply concerned with the poet's relationship to community and whom Klein saw as a kind of alter ego. Within a year of the completion of the Bialik translations, Klein returned to original poetry with a series of political satires represented, in this volume, by excerpts from 'Barricade Smith: His Speeches' and from 'Of Castles in Spain.' On the whole, neither Klein's imagination nor his intellect seems very fully engaged in these poems. As he turns restlessly from one issue to another – unemployment, the threat of war, the rise of fascism – he seems to be floundering in a search for something to say, some position to take, some social role to play, that would genuinely answer his imaginative needs.

In 1938, Klein took on the editorship of the *Canadian Jewish Chronicle*, a position he held until his final breakdown in 1955. The drain on his time and energy during these years (when he also continued to practise law and took up a new position as speech-writer and public relations adviser to Samuel Bronfman) must have been substantial. Paradoxically, however, it was precisely at this time that Klein began to enter into the most productive stage of his career. In the late thirties, Klein had been as aware as anyone of the terrible events which were overtaking the Jews of Europe, but his new role as editor of the *Chronicle* demanded of him a more intense scrutiny of these events than ever before. Thus, his journalistic responsibilities, though in some ways a burdensome distraction from his poetry, forced upon him a new approach to his theme of community, an approach for which he had searched in vain over the previous half-dozen years. They forced upon him, as well, a new and heightened sense of his responsibility as a poet.

The first signs of these new developments were two long dramatic monologues, 'Childe Harold's Pilgrimage' (not included in this volume), which appeared just as Klein took on his editorship of the *Chronicle*, and '*In Re* Solomon Warshawer,' which dates from about a year later. In these poems Klein confronts the contemporary situation of the Jewish people, and attempts to place it in a broader historical perspective. Soon after completing '*In Re*,' Klein began writing a series of poems which he identified as psalms. In the most successful of these poems, he effectively draws on the heightened diction and imagery of the Bible while maintaining a sense of very personal urgency in the face of the evils he saw as threatening to engulf, first the Jewish community, and then the world. Consumed by his prophetic task, he often feels that he stands alone, and he sometimes confesses to fears of madness and death. Although the psalms are, at times, marred by a note of forced rhetoric, in the best of them the immediacy of Klein's lonely confrontation with evil gives rise to a pathos and intensity that are new in his work.

The evils of Nazism form the subject of a second group of poems, the ballads which Klein began at about the time he had completed the psalms. In choosing the popular ballad form, Klein perhaps hoped to reach a wider audience than he had with the more personal and more demanding psalms. But, on the whole, the ballads are less successful than the psalms; the tension between their grim subject matter and their almost jaunty verse, often bordering on doggerel, is, in most cases, jarring rather than effective.

Similar difficulties would arise with Klein's satire *The Hitleriad*, which he appears to have begun early in 1942, probably not long after he had completed the last of the ballads. Taken as a whole, *The Hitleriad* is, without a doubt, the least successful of Klein's major works. It is crippled by Klein's understandable inability to identify in any way with the characters he is satirizing, an inability to see them as participating in the same human community as himself. Hitler and his henchmen had placed themselves so far outside the pale of humanity that Klein can present them only as grotesques, contemptible but, somehow, not completely serious or real. In the end, the effect is trivializing, and the bombastic, hectoring tone of much of the poem reflects the fundamental flaw in Klein's relationship with his subject.

The period immediately following the completion of *The Hitleriad* was a painful one for Klein. None of his published volumes – *Hath Not a Jew ...*, *Poems*, and *The Hitleriad* – had received the kind of response that he had hoped for, and this fact, no doubt, contributed to a searching reappraisal of his sense of himself and of his social role as poet which he undertook in the early forties. The experience was not a pleasant one, but it was to lead to his finest poetry.

One aspect of this reappraisal was Klein's deepening awareness of himself as a modernist, stimulated by his involvement with the group of writers associated with *Preview* (Patrick Anderson, P.K. Page, F.R. Scott) and *First Statement* (Irving Layton, John Sutherland, Louis Dudek). These writers, through their often unsparing criticism, as well as their example, helped Klein to complete a long process that had begun years earlier, when he was first introduced to modernism by the McGill Group. If Klein was not ready, in the twenties, to fully accept what the McGill Group had to offer him, his profoundly troubling experiences in the intervening years had made him much more sympathetic to modernism as a response to historical and social crisis. By the early forties Klein had come to terms with modern poetry more fully than he had ever done before, and he had developed a more contemporary voice – tougher, more colloquial, more ironic – which was less immediately accessible than in the past, but almost entirely free of the poeticisms and overwrought rhetoric that had blunted the impact of much of his earlier verse.

There was one other development at this period which was to have a profound effect on the rest of Klein's career. Sometime in the early forties, Klein began to develop a keen interest in dialectical modes of thought, and to see his role as a poet in dialectical terms. The unrelentingly negative historical events of the previous decade were now taken up into a dialectical vision (owing more to the Kabbalah than to Marx), in which negation, in the form of social and spiritual fragmentation, was seen as ultimately negating itself, and leading to the achievement of a higher synthesis. Klein's major prose statement of this vision is *The Second Scroll*; his major poetic statement is 'Portrait of the Poet as Landscape,' the poem to which all of Klein's poetry of the early forties can be seen to have led, and out of which all of the poetry of the late forties can be seen to have proceeded.

Klein's journey towards 'Portrait,' in the early forties, is the best-documented episode of his career. Most of the relevant documents (which have been published in the *Notebooks* volume of the *Collected Works*) consist of incomplete but often highly finished writings which blur the boundaries between diary, autobiography, fiction, and poetry. In this intriguing body of work, we see Klein struggling to come to terms with a growing sense of futility and alienation. The poetry of this period, much of it unpublished in Klein's lifetime, is dark indeed. There is a pervasive sense of disgust, and several of the poems, such as 'Les Vespasiennes,' are set in a sordid urban landscape which bears little resemblance to the Montreal Klein was to celebrate a few years later. It is only in 'Portrait of the Poet as Landscape,' which he began at the very end of this period, that Klein was able to give form to his sense of negation, and to look beyond it, if only tentatively, to the dialectical vision of a 'synthesis olympic, fields where no negatives can live,' as an early version of the poem has it.

In 'Portrait of the Poet as Landscape' Klein tentatively works his way through to the conviction that the rejection which he has suffered at society's hands is a necessary stage in the education of his imagination. When and if this process reaches completion, he will be able to assume a function which is, in true dialectical fashion, both new and old, a function which was once the ultimate aim of the poetic craft, but which most modern poets have long since abandoned. Like the poets of old who 'unrolled our culture from [their] scroll,' he will give utterance to those values which are essential to the life of any true community:

> To find a new function for the déclassé craft
> archaic like the fletcher's; to make a new thing;
> to say the word that will become sixth sense;
> perhaps by necessity and indirection bring
> new forms to life, anonymously, new creeds ...

Impressive as this vision is, we are never allowed to dismiss the possibility that the poet's vision may be a self-aggrandizing illusion. With hindsight, we cannot help but think of the close of the poem, with the poet 'at the bottom of the sea,' as a tragic foreshadowing of the 'unnegateable negation' (to use Klein's own phrase) that was to overtake him in another ten years. However, the immediate effect of 'Portrait' was undoubtedly a liberating one for Klein. Having established the poet's role as 'bring[ing] new forms to life' 'by necessity and indirection,' he then set out to fulfil this program, as completely as he was ever to fulfil it, in the poems of the next few years which went to make up *The Rocking Chair and Other Poems* (1948).

In this collection, Klein is freed by an act of 'necessity and indirection' to explore, more profoundly than ever before, the theme of community which had always been at the centre of his major works. The treatment of community in *The Rocking Chair* clearly had a deep personal meaning for Klein. The Québécois inevitably recalled to him his own community: he recognized in them a similar devotion to language, family, and religion, stubbornly maintained in the face of a history of betrayal and oppression. If these similarities enabled him to draw on his personal experience to celebrate a living community, they also enabled him to confront, with a freedom denied him in his explicitly Jewish poems, the limitations of community as he had suffered them, a crippling narrowness and fearfulness in the face of the unknown. '*Invoke, revoke*' is the song of the rocking chair in the title poem of the volume, and it seems to express Klein's own ambivalent feelings, his sense that as the community gives it takes away, and that the artist who seeks to invoke the values of his community must also revoke much that is essential to his individual creativity before the community will fully accept him as one of its own. The strongest of the *Rocking Chair* poems – poems such as 'The Rocking Chair' or 'Political Meeting' – rise above specifics of time and place, and stand as profoundly dialectical studies of the power of community, any community, for both good and evil. There is much in *The Rocking Chair* that one can trace to the influence of various modern writers, but the mixture of irony and affection, sharp observation and imaginative elaboration, that plays over Klein's images of community is peculiarly his own.

The Rocking Chair was the best received of Klein's books; it was immediately recognized as his finest work, and won him the Governor General's Award, as well as enthusiastic praise in Quebec for its accu-

xviii / Editors' Introduction

racy and sensitivity. But, surprisingly, it represented Klein's last major body of poetry. It may be that the particular vein of poetry represented by the *Rocking Chair* poems had become exhausted, and that, before he could strike another vein, he became involved in a swirl of distracting activities that made the writing of poetry impossible. Soon after the publication of *The Rocking Chair*, Klein ran for the CCF in the federal riding of Cartier. After a devastating defeat, he was sent by the Canadian Jewish Congress to Israel on a fact-finding tour. When he returned, he immediately began work on *The Second Scroll* which drew on his experiences in Israel, and set out on an exhausting lecture tour on behalf of the United Jewish Appeal. Although, in the years that followed, Klein did not undertake any major poetic projects, he did continue to devote some of his energy to poetry, and the work that he produced in the early fifties provides ample evidence that, whatever the cause of his final silence, it was not a loss of his poetic powers. From this period date some very impressive revisions to a number of his most important poems (in particular, a substantial section added to 'In Re Solomon Warshawer,' which is one of his finest achievements) and new translations of Bialik, which are among the most moving poems he ever wrote, far superior to the translations of the thirties. However, the major projects of the period were in prose; they are Klein's final word on his relationship to his community and on his ambitions as a poet, and it is to them that we must turn for an insight into the pressures that may have contributed to the silence which was soon to follow.

In Klein's last major prose works, we hear the voice of a man who feels himself not merely cut off from any genuine relationship with his community, but irremediably so. The dialectical vision of the poet and his community which Klein had developed as a response to his sense of negation no longer holds. 'The unnegateable negation! ... I write from its very centre and vacuum,' says Czernik in the short story 'Letter from Afar,' and, at times, Klein seems determined to demonstrate, once and for all, that the negation is unnegateable, as he rewrites and subverts the great statements of hope that grew out of the dialectical vision of the forties. This process is especially striking in his late essay 'The Bible's Archetypical Poet,' in which Klein recasts 'Portrait of the Poet as Landscape' in terms of an allegorical reading of the story of Joseph, retaining the basic pattern of exile and return, but significantly darkening its mood. The poet, represented by Joseph, is now seen as the victim of a murderous conspiracy, 'a design which repeats itself down through the ages' and which no dialectic has the power, ultimately, to transform. Klein continued to work on his prose writings until about 1953, but, by then, his increasing mental instability, manifesting itself in feelings of persecution and in several suicide attempts, seems to have made sustained work impossible. Not long after, he fell into a silence from which he was never to recover.

To 'bring new forms to life ... new creeds' – few poets have set themselves such high ambitions and fewer still have achieved them. Klein was aware that the redemptive social role that he sought to assume on behalf of his community was no longer fully possible in the twentieth century, if it had ever really been possible. Yet, unwilling to accept anything less for the 'déclassé craft archaic like the fletcher's,' he struggled relentlessly against this awareness. It may be that the end of Klein's career was hastened by the stress of his inner struggle, but it is to this struggle, and to the ambitions that inspired it, that we owe some of the most moving poems of our time.

TEXTUAL NOTE

The *Selected Poems* takes its place alongside two other collections that have served somewhat different purposes. A *Collected Poems*, compiled by Miriam Waddington, appeared in 1974, and has long been out of print. It included only previously published poems, many in defective versions, and contained no annotations or textual apparatus. Zailig Pollock's critical edition of the *Complete Poems*, which appeared in 1990, includes all of Klein's poems both published and unpublished. Thoroughly annotated and filling two hardcover volumes, it was aimed primarily at a scholarly audience.

In putting this volume together, the three editors have tried to balance two important requirements: intrinsic merit and representativeness. We take ultimate responsibility for the final results, but in the process of arriving at our selection we consulted many colleagues, including the members of the A.M. Klein Research and Publication Committee and its editorial board. We have also taken into consideration the judgments that have emerged during six decades of anthologizing and criticism of Klein's poetry. As a result of this process, it became clear that there are fifteen or twenty poems which are widely recognized as constituting the core of Klein's achievement: poems such as 'Out of the Pulver and the Polished Lens,' 'Heirloom,' 'Now We Will Suffer Loss of Memory,' 'A Psalm Touching Genealogy,' 'Portrait of the Poet as Landscape,' 'The Rocking Chair,' 'Political Meeting,' 'For the Sisters of the Hotel Dieu,' and 'Elegy' were on virtually everyone's list. Beyond that it was clear that there were almost as many Kleins as readers – the Jewish, the Canadian, and the multicultural Klein; the religious Klein and the secular Klein; the traditional and the modernist Klein; the satirical, the sentimental, and the humorous Klein; the radical Klein; the confessional Klein; the prophetic Klein; the tragic Klein. We believe that this selection represents as many of these Kleins as possible and does so through works, or extracts from works, which are successful in their own right, regardless of whatever aspect of Klein they are seen to represent. Individuals familiar with Klein's work will no doubt question some of our choices, but we are confident that readers interested in experiencing the full range of Klein's poetic achievement will be well served by this selection.

The texts published here are all based on the *Complete Poems*. A couple of corrections have been made. These are recorded in the notes to the poems in question.

The *Complete Poems* follows a strictly chronological order of arrangement, whereas in the present volume an attempt has been made to give some shape to the whole, mainly by respecting the patterns and groupings to be found in the collections published during Klein's own lifetime. We also include in this selection three translations of poems by Chaim Nachman Bialik, produced at the very end of Klein's career. These translations, apart from being fine poems in their own right, provide a unique insight into Klein's final years when he had almost entirely ceased to write original poetry.

Textual and explanatory notes are based on the much fuller notes in the *Complete Poems*. See pages 153–4 for a more detailed account of the notes.

SELECTED POEMS

Poems

Portraits of a Minyan

Landlord

He is a learned man, adept
   At softening the rigid.
Purblind, he scans the *rashi* script,
   His very nose is digit.

He justifies his point of view
   With verses pedagogic;
His thumb is double-jointed through
   Stressing a doubtful logic.

He quotes the Commentaries, yea,
   To Tau from Aleph, –
But none the less, his tenants pay,
   Or meet the bailiff.

Pintele Yid

Agnostic, he would never tire
   To cauterize the orthodox;
But he is here, by paradox,
   To say the *Kaddish* for his sire.

Reb Abraham

Reb Abraham, the jolly,
Avowed the gloomy face
Unpardonable folly,
Unworthy of his race.

When God is served in revel
By all his joyous Jews,
(He says) the surly devil
Stands gloomy at the news.

Reb Abraham loved Torah,
If followed by a feast:
A milah-banquet, or a
Schnapps to drink, at least.

On Sabbath-nights, declaring
God's praises, who did cram
The onion and the herring?
Fat-cheeked Reb Abraham.

On Ninth of Ab, who aided
The youngsters in their game
Of throwing burrs, as they did,
In wailing beards? The same.

And who on Purim came in
To help the urchins, when
They rattled at foul Haman?
Reb Abraham again.

On all feasts of rejoicing
Reb Abraham's thick soles
Stamped pious metres, voicing
Laudation of the scrolls.

Averring that in heaven
One more Jew had been crowned,
Reb Abraham drank even
On cemetery-ground.

And at Messiah's greeting,
Reb Abraham's set plan
Is to make goodly eating
Of roast leviathan.

When God is served in revel
By all His joyous Jews,
(He says) the surly devil
Stands gloomy at the news.

Shadchan

Cupid in a caftan
    Slowly scrutinizes
Virgins and rich widows,
    And other lesser prizes.

Cupid strokes his chin, and
    Values legs at so much,
So much for straight noses,
    Cupid pays love homage.

What's a squinted eye, or
    What's a halting stutter,
When her father offers
    More than bread and butter?

Cupid whets his arrows –
    Golden, golden rocket!
Aims, not at the bosom,
    Aims them at the pocket.

Cupid in a caftan
   Disregards the flowery
Speech of moon-mad lovers.
   Cupid talks of dowry.

Sophist

When will there be another such brain?
Never; unless he rise again,
Unless Reb Simcha rise once more
To juggle syllogistic lore.

One placed a pin upon a page
Of Talmud print, whereat the sage
Declared what holy word was writ
Two hundred pages under it!

That skull replete with pilpul tricks
Has long returned to its matrix,
Where worms split hair, where Death confutes
The hope the all-too-hopeful moots.

But I think that in Paradise
Reb Simcha, with his twinkling eyes,
Interprets, in some song-spared nook,
To God the meaning of His book.

Reader of the Scroll

Divinely he sang the scriptured note;
He twisted sound, intoned the symbol,
Made music sally, slow or nimble,
From out his heart and through his throat.

For in a single breath to hiss
The ten outrageous names of those

Who on the Persian gallows rose –
Oh, this was pleasure, joyance this!

Sweet Singer

O what would David say,
Young David in the fields,
Singing in Bethlehem,
Were he to hear this day
Old Mendel slowly hum
His sweetest songs,
Old Mendel, who being poor,
Cannot through charity
Atone his wrongs,
And being ignorant,
Cannot in learned wise
Win Paradise,
Old Mendel who begs Heaven as his alms
By iterating and re-iterating psalms?

Junk-Dealer

All week his figure mottles
    The city lanes,
Hawking his rags and bottles
    In quaint refrains.

But on the High, the Holy
    Days, he is lord;
And being lord, earth wholly,
    Gladly is abhorred.

While litanies are clamored,
    His loud voice brags
A Hebrew most ungrammared.
    He sells God rags.

His Was an Open Heart

His was an open heart, a lavish hand,
His table ever set for any guest:
A rabbi passing from a foreign land,
A holy man, a beggar, all found rest
Beneath his roof; even a Gentile saw
A welcome at the door, a face that smiled.
The chillest heart beneath his warmth would thaw.
And for these deeds, God blessed him that he saw
The cradle never emptied of its child.

And the Man Moses Was Meek

This little Jew
Homunculus
Found four ells too
Capacious.

He never spoke,
Save in his prayer;
He bore his yoke
As it were air.

He knew not sin.
He even blessed
The spider in
His corner-nest.

The meek may trust
That in his tomb
He will turn dust
To save some room.

Out of the Pulver and the Polished Lens

I

The paunchy sons of Abraham
Spit on the maculate streets of Amsterdam,
Showing Spinoza, Baruch *alias* Benedict,
He and his God are under interdict.

Ah, what theology there is in spatted spittle,
And in anathema what sacred prose
Winnowing the fact from the suppose!
Indeed, what better than these two things can whittle
The scabrous heresies of Yahweh's foes,
Informing the breast where Satan gloats and crows
That saving it leave false doctrine, jot and tittle,
No vigilant thumb will leave its orthodox nose?
What better than ram's horn blown,
And candles blown out by maledictory breath,
Can bring the wanderer back to his very own,
The infidel back to his faith?

Nothing, unless it be that from the ghetto
A soldier of God advance to teach the creed,
Using as rod the irrefutable stiletto.

II

Uriel da Costa
Flightily ranted
Heresies one day,
Next day recanted.

Rabbi and bishop
Each vies to smuggle

Soul of da Costa
Out of its struggle.

Confessional hears his
Glib paternoster;
Synagogue sees his
Penitent posture.

What is the end of
This catechism?
Bullet brings dogma
That suffers no schism.

III

Malevolent scorpions befoul thy chambers,
O my heart; they scurry across its floor,
Leaving the slimy vestiges of doubt.

Banish memento of the vermin; let
No scripture on the wall affright you; no
Ghost of da Costa; no, nor any threat.
Ignore, O heart, even as didst ignore
The bribe of florins jingling in the purse.

IV

Jehovah is factotum of the rabbis;
And Christ endures diurnal Calvary;
Polyglot God is exiled to the churches;
Synods tell God to be or not to be.

The Lord within his vacuum of heaven
Discourses his domestic policies,
With angels who break off their loud hosannas
To help him phrase infallible decrees.

Soul of Spinoza, Baruch Spinoza bids you
Forsake the god suspended in mid-air,
Seek you that other Law, and let Jehovah
Play his game of celestial solitaire.

V

    Reducing providence to theorems, the horrible atheist compiled
such lore that proved, like proving two and two make four, that
in the crown of God we all are gems. From glass and dust of glass
he brought to light, out of the pulver and the polished lens, the
prism and the flying mote; and hence the infinitesimal and
infinite.
    Is it a marvel, then, that he forsook the abracadabra of the
synagogue, and holding with timelessness a duologue, deciphered
a new scripture in the book? Is it a marvel that he left old fraud
for passion intellectual of God?

VI

Unto the crown of bone cry *Suzerain*!
Do genuflect before the jewelled brain!
Lavish the homage of the vassal; let
The blood grow heady with strong epithet;
O cirque of the Cabbalist! O proud skull!
Of alchemy O crucible!
Sanctum sanctorum; grottoed hermitage
Where sits the bearded sage!
O golden bowl of Koheleth! and of fate
O hourglass within the pate!
Circling, O planet in the occiput!
O Macrocosm, sinew-shut!
Yea, and having uttered this loud *Te Deum*
Ye have been singularly dumb.

VII

I am weak before the wind; before the sun
  I faint; I lose my strength;
I am utterly vanquished by a star;
  I go to my knees, at length

Before the song of a bird; before
  The breath of spring or fall
I am lost; before these miracles
  I am nothing at all.

VIII

Lord, accept my hallelujahs; look not askance at these my
petty words; unto perfection a fragment makes its prayer.

For thou art the world, and I am part thereof; thou art the
blossom and I its fluttering petal.

I behold thee in all things, and in all things: lo, it is myself;
I look into the pupil of thine eye, it is my very countenance I
see.

Thy glory fills the earth; it is the earth; the noise of the deep,
the moving of many waters, is it not thy voice aloud, O Lord,
aloud that all may hear?

The wind through the almond-trees spreads the fragrance of
thy robes; the turtle-dove twittering utters diminutives of thy
love; at the rising of the sun I behold thy countenance.

Yea, and in the crescent moon, thy little finger's finger-nail.

If I ascend up into heaven, thou art there; If I make my bed in
hell, behold thou art there.

Thou art everywhere; a pillar to thy sanctuary is every blade of
grass.

Wherefore I said to the wicked, Go to the ant, thou sluggard,
seek thou an audience with God.

On the swift wings of a star, even on the numb legs of a snail,
thou dost move, O Lord.

A babe in swaddling clothes laughs at the sunbeams on the

door's lintel; the sucklings play with thee; with thee Kopernik
holds communion through a lens.

I am thy son, O Lord, and brother to all that lives am I.

The flowers of the field, they are kith and kin to me; the lily my
sister, the rose is my blood and flesh.

Even as the stars in the firmament move, so does my inward
heart, and even as the moon draws the tides in the bay, so does it
the blood in my veins.

For thou art the world, and I am part thereof;

Howbeit, even in dust I am resurrected; and even in decay I live
again.

IX

Think of Spinoza, then, not as you think
Of Shabbathai Zvi who for a time of life
Took to himself the Torah for a wife,
And underneath the silken canopy
Made public: Thou art hallowed unto me.

Think of Spinoza, rather, plucking tulips
Within the garden of Mynheer, forgetting
Dutchmen and Rabbins, and consumptive fretting,
Plucking his tulips in the Holland sun,
Remembering the thought of the Adored,
Spinoza, gathering flowers for the One,
The ever-unwedded lover of the Lord.

Design for Mediaeval Tapestry

Somewhere a hungry muzzle rooted.
The frogs among the sedges croaked.
Into the night a screech-owl hooted.

A clawed mouse squeaked and struggled, choked.
The wind pushed antlers through the bushes.
Terror stalked through the forest, cloaked.

Was it a robber broke the hushes?
Was it a knight in armoured thews,
Walking in mud, and bending rushes?

Was it a provost seeking Jews?
The Hebrews shivered; their teeth rattled;
Their beards glittered with gelid dews.

Gulped they their groans, for silence tattled;
They crushed their sighs, for quiet heard;
They had their thoughts on Israel battled

By pagan and by Christian horde.
They moved their lips in pious anguish.
They made no sound. They never stirred.

*

Reb Zadoc Has Memories.

Reb Zadoc's brain is a German town:
Hermits come from lonely grottos
Preaching the right for Jews to drown;

Soldiers who vaunt their holy mottos
Stroking the cross that is a sword;
Barons plotting in cabal sottos;

A lady spitting on the abhorred.
The market-place and faggot-fire –
A hangman burning God's true word;

A clean-shaved traitor-Jew; a friar
Dropping his beads upon his paunch;
The heavens speared by a Gothic spire;

The Judengasse and its stench
Rising from dark and guarded alleys
Where Jew is neighboured to harlot-wench

Perforce ecclesiastic malice;
The exile-booths of Jacob where
Fat burghers come to pawn a chalice

While whistling a Jew-hating air;
Peasants regarding Jews and seeking
The hooves, the tail, the horn-crowned hair;

And target for a muddy streaking,
The yellow badge upon the breast,
The vengeance of a papal wreaking;

The imposts paid for this fine crest;
Gay bailiffs serving writs of seizure;
Even the town fool and his jest –

Stroking his beard with slowly leisure,
A beard that was but merely down,
Rubbing his palms with gloating pleasure,

Counting fictitious crown after crown.
Reb Zadoc's brain is a torture-dungeon;
Reb Zadoc's brain is a German town.

Reb Daniel Shochet Reflects.

The toad seeks out its mud; the mouse discovers
The nibbled hole; the sparrow owns its nest;
About the blind mole earthy shelter hovers.

The louse avows the head where it is guest;
Even the roach calls some dark fent his dwelling.
But Israel owns a sepulchre, at best.

Nahum-this-also-is-for-the-good Ponders.

The wrath of God is just. His punishment
Is most desirable. The flesh of Jacob
Implores the scourge. For this was Israel meant.

Below we have no life. But we will wake up
Beyond, where popes will lave our feet, where princes
Will heed our insignificantest hiccup.

The sins of Israel only blood-shed rinses.
We teach endurance. Lo, we are not spent.
We die, we live; at once we are three tenses.

Our skeletons are bibles; flesh is rent
Only to prove a thesis, stamp a moral.
The rack prepared: for this was Israel meant.

Isaiah Epicure Avers.

Seek reasons; rifle your theology;
Philosophize; expend your dialectic;
Decipher and translate God's diary;

Discover causes, primal and eclectic;
I cannot; all I know is this:
That pain doth render flesh most sore and hectic;

That lance-points prick; that scorched bones hiss;
That thumbscrews agonize, and that a martyr
Is mad if he considers these things bliss.

Job Reviles.

God is grown ancient. He no longer hears.
He has been deafened by his perfect thunders.
With clouds for cotton he has stopped his ears.

The Lord is purblind; and his heaven sunders
Him from the peccadillos of this earth.
He meditates his youth; he dreams; he wonders.

His cherubs have acquired beards and girth.
They cannot move to do his bidding. Even
The angels yawn. Satan preserves his mirth.

How long, O Lord, will Israel's heart be riven?
How long will we cry to a dotard God
To let us keep the breath that He has given?

How long will you sit on your throne, and nod?

Judith Makes Comparisons.

Judith had heard a troubadour
Singing beneath a castle-turret
Of truth, chivàlry, and honoùr,
Of virtue, and of gallant merit, –
Judith had heard a troubadour
Lauding the parfait knightly spirit,
Singing beneath the ivied wall.
The cross-marked varlet Judith wrestled
Was not like these at all, at all ...

Ezekiel the Simple Opines.

If we will fast for forty days; if we
Will read the psalms thrice over; if we offer
To God some blossom-bursting litany,

And to the poor a portion of the coffer;
If we don sack-cloth, and let ashes rain
Upon our heads, despite the boor and scoffer,

Certes, these things will never be again.

Solomon Talmudi Considers His Life.

Rather that these blood-thirsty pious vandals,
Bearing sable in heart, and gules on arm,
Had made me ready for the cerement-candles,

Than that they should have taken my one charm
Against mortality, my exegesis:
The script that gave the maggot the alarm.

Jews would have crumpled Rashi's simple thesis
On reading this, and Ibn Ezra's version;
Maimonides they would have torn to pieces.

For here, in black and white, by God's conversion,
I had plucked secrets from the pentateuch,
And gathered strange arcana from dispersion,

The essence and quintessence of the book!
Green immortality smiled out its promise –
I hung my gaberdine on heaven's hook.

Refuting Duns, and aquinatic Thomas,
Confounding Moslems, proving the one creed
A simple sentence broken by no commas,

I thought to win myself eternal meed,
I thought to move the soul with sacred lever
And lift the heart to God in very deed.

Ah, woe is me, and to my own endeavour,
That on that day they burned my manuscript,
And lost my name, for certain, and for ever!

Simeon Takes Hints from His Environs.

Heaven is God's grimace at us on high.
This land is a cathedral; speech, its sermon.
The moon is a rude gargoyle in the sky.

The leaves rustle. Come, who will now determine
Whether this be the wind, or priestly robes.
The frogs croak out ecclesiastic German,

Whereby our slavish ears have punctured lobes.
The stars are mass-lamps on a lofty altar;
Even the angels are Judaeophobes.

There is one path; in it I shall not falter.
Let me rush to the bosom of the state
And church, grasp lawyer-code and monkish psalter,

And being Christianus Simeon, late
Of Jewry, have much comfort and salvation –
Salvation in this life, at any rate.

Esther Hears Echoes of His Voice.

How sweetly did he sing grace after meals!
He now is silent. He has fed on sorrow.
He lies where he is spurned by faithless heels.

His voice was honey. Lovers well might borrow
Warmth from his words. His words were musical,
Making the night so sweet, so sweet the morrow!

Can I forget the tremors of his call?
Can kiddush benediction be forgotten?
His blood is spilled like wine. The earth is sharp with gall.

As soothing as the promises begotten
Of penitence and love; as lovely as
The turtle-dove; as soft as snow in cotton,

Whether he lulled a child or crooned the laws,
And sacred as the eighteen prayers, so even
His voice. His voice was so. His voice that was ...

     *

The burgher sleeps beside his wife, and dreams
Of human venery, and Hebrew quarry.
His sleep contrives him many little schemes.

There will be Jews, dead, moribund and gory;
There will be booty; there will be dark maids,
And there will be a right good spicy story ...

     *

The moon has left her vigil. Lucifer fades.
Whither shall we betake ourselves, O Father?
Whither to flee? And where to find our aids?

The wrath of people is like foam and lather,
Risen against us. Wherefore, Lord, and why?
The winds assemble; the cold and hot winds gather

To scatter us. They do not heed our cry.
The sun rises and leaps the red horizon,
And like a bloodhound swoops across the sky.

Haggadah

Etching

The sky is dotted like th' unleavened bread,
The moon a golden platter in the sky.
Old midget Jews, with meditated tread,
Hands clasped behind, and body stooped ahead,
Creep from the synagogue and stare on high
Upon a golden platter in a dotted sky.

Once in a Year

Once in a year this comes to pass:
My father is a king in a black skull cap,
My mother is a queen in a brown perruque,
A princess my sister, a lovely lass,
My brother a prince, and I a duke.

Silver and plate, and fine cut-glass
Brought from the cupboards that hid them till now
Banquet King David's true lineage here.
Once in a year this comes to pass,
Once in a long unroyal year.

Black Decalogue

Compute the plagues; your little finger dip
In spittle of the grape, and at each pest
Shake off the drop with the vindictive zest:
Thus first: The Nile – a gash; then frogs that skip
Upon the princess' coverlet; the rip
Made by dark nails that seek the itching guest;
The plague of murrained carcasses; the pest;

Full boils that stud the Ethiop, leg to lip.
The guerdon of hot hail, the fists of God;
The swarm of locusts nibbling Egypt clean;
Thick darkness oozing from out Moses' rod;
And first-born slain, the mighty and the mean;
Compute these plagues that fell on Egypt's sod, –
Then add: In Goshen these were never seen.

The Bitter Dish

This is the bread of our affliction, this
The symbol of the clay that built Rameses,
And that horseradish – root of bitterness,
And you, my brethren, yea,
You are the afflicted, the embittered, and the clay.

Song

Fill the silver goblet;
Make open the door-way;
Let there be no sob; let
Elijah come our way.

And let him come singing,
Announcing as nigh a
Redemption, and drinking
The health of Messiah!

Chad Gadyah

This is a curious plot
Devised for eager riddling:
My father had a kidling
For two good zuzim bought.

Graymalkin ate it; and
A dog munched sleek Graymalkin,
Whereat a Rod did stalk in
Beating his reprimand

Upon the Dog's spine. Came
Red Fire, and did sputter
His wrath on Rod; came Water
And sizzling, quenched the flame.

And down a bovine throat
Went Water, which throat, tickled
By pious Shochet, trickled
Red blood upon his coat.

The Angel of Death flew
And smote the Shochet; whereat
The Lord gave him his merit –
The Lord the Angel slew.

In that strange portal whence
All things come, they re-enter;
Of all things God is centre,
God is circumference.

This is a curious plot
Devised for eager riddling:
My father had a kidling
For two good zuzim bought.

The Still Small Voice

The candles splutter; and the kettle hums;
The heirloomed clock enumerates the tribes;
Upon the wine-stained table-cloth lie crumbs
Of matzoh whose wide scattering describes
Jews driven in far lands upon this earth.

The kettle hums; the candles splutter; and
Winds whispering from shutters tell re-birth
Of beauty rising in an eastern land,
Of paschal sheep driven in cloudy droves;
Of almond-blossoms colouring the breeze;
Of vineyards upon verdant terraces;
Of golden globes in orient orange-groves.
And those assembled at the table dream
Of small schemes that an April wind doth scheme,
And cry from out the sleep assailing them:
Jerusalem, next year! Next year, Jerusalem!

Plumaged Proxy

O rooster, circled over my brother's head,
If you had foresight you would see a beard
Pluck little feathers from your neck, a blade
Slit open your alarum, and a thumb
Press down your gullet, rendering it dumb.
My brother sends you to a land of shade,
Hebraically curses your new home,
And sets his sins upon your ruddy comb,
Atonement for the gifts of Satan's trade.
O rooster in a vortex of repentance,
Proxy of my little brother's soul,
You speed into a land where death pays toll;
Where no sun rises to evoke a crow
    You go.
Be you not lonesome. I will send you thither
Each year a new companion for each year
My brother lets his peccadilloes wither.
Be you intrepid, therefore; do not fear.
May six score roosters in the course of time
Be cooped with you upon your nether stage.
And may my brother live to a ripe age.

Scribe

I

The black phylacteries about his arm
Impress the first initial of God's name
Upon the skin, encircled by this charm.
The Sheen of Shaddai intricately drawn
Into the flesh sets bone and blood aflame.
The heart beats out the tetragrammaton.

II

Let heathenesse seek refuge in its steel;
Let pagandom invest its coat of mail;
This prayer-shawl is armour to this Jew!
Satan endures its pendules as a flail;
Demons are frighted by its white and blue;
And Lilith knows a hauberk she can not undo.

III

His eyes are two black blots of ink.
The thin hairs of his beard
Are symbols of the script revered;
His broad brow is the margin of a parchment page,
Clean for the commentaries of age.

IV

Having shaped a chapter of the Holy Writ,
Having reached the name of God,
Let no hair fallen from his beard unhallow it.

Let no imp alcoved in a finger nail
Play his unsacred fraud.
Therefore let living water wash his right hand clean,
Drowning the satans on his palm, unseen and seen.

V

And after three score years and ten,
He will have raised three pentateuchs
Aloft to be the praise of men;
His eyes will then be water, his bones hooks.
His fingers will not write again.

VI

He will descend unto that other ark
Which has no curtains save an empty shroud.
And there the slimy exegetes will mark
Exegesis upon the parchment-browed.

VII

But the true essence, joyous as a lark,
Will settle on God's wrist, devoutly proud!

A Benediction

O bridegroom eager for the bride,
O white-veiled bride,
May love be on your pillow; may
The quiet turtledove preside

Your sweet consortments night and day;
May the months be fat for you; bask
  In the sun; love in the moon; let bread
  Be never wanting from your table,
    Wine from your cask,
    Warmth from your bed.
O let the almond flourish on your tree,
O let the grape grow big, and full of juice
  And of the perfect shape:
Let nine months grow diffuse, and wax and grow diffuse,
  And let the first-born be.

Would That Three Centuries Past Had Seen Us Born

Would that three centuries past had seen us born!
When gallants brought a continent on a chart
To turreted ladies waiting their return.
Then had my gifts in truth declared my heart!
From foreign coasts, over tempestuous seas,
I would have brought a gold-caged parrakeet;
Gems from some painted tribe; the Sultan's keys;
Bright coronets; and placed them at your feet.
Yea, on the high seas raised a sombre flag,
And singed unwelcome beards, and made for shore
With precious stones, and coins in many a bag
To proffer you. These deeds accomplished, or
I would have been a humble thin-voiced Jew
Hawking old clo'es in ghetto lanes, for you.

These Northern Stars Are Scarabs in My Eyes

These northern stars are scarabs in my eyes.
Not any longer can I suffer them.
I will to Palestine. We will arise
And seek the towers of Jerusalem.
Make ready to board ship. Say farewells. Con
Your Hebrew primer; supple be your tongue
To speak the crisp words baked beneath the sun,
The sinuous phrases by the sweet-singer sung.
At last, my bride, in our estate you'll wear
Sweet orange-blossoms in an orange grove.
There will be white doves fluttering in the air,
And in the meadows our contented drove,
Sheep on the hills, and in the trees, my love,
There will be sparrows twittering *Mazel Tov*.

Now We Will Suffer Loss of Memory

Now we will suffer loss of memory;
We will forget the tongue our mothers knew;
We will munch ham, and guzzle milk thereto,
And this on hallowed fast-days, purposely ...
Abe will elude his base-nativity.
The kike will be a phantom; we will rue
Our bearded ancestry, my nasal cue,
And like the gentiles we will strive to be.
Our recompense – emancipation-day.
We will have friend where once we had a foe.
Impugning epithets will glance astray.
To gentile parties we will proudly go;

And Christians, anecdoting us, will say:
'Mr. and Mrs. Klein – the Jews, you know ...'

Saturday Night

It being no longer Sabbath, angels scrawl
The stars upon the sky; and Main Street thrives.
The butcher-shops are as so many hives,
And full is every delicatessen stall.
Obese Jewesses, wheeling triplets, crawl
Along the gibbering thoroughfare. Fat wives
Lead little husbands, while their progeny dives
Among this corpulence in shouting frisky sprawl.
The whole street quivers with a million hums.
Hebraic arms tell jokes that are not funny.
Upon the corner stand the pool-room bums.
Most valiantly girl-taggers smile for money.
From out a radio loud-speaker comes:
O, Eli, Eli, lama zabachthani!

Dialogue

The two shawl-covered grannies, buying fish,
Discuss the spices of the Sabbath dish.

They laud old-country dainties; each one bans
The heathen foods the moderns eat from cans.

They get to talking of the golden land,
Each phrase of theirs couching a reprimand ...

Says one: I hate these lofty buildings, I
Long for a piece of unencircled sky ...

I do not know the tramway system, so
I walk and curse the traffic as I go.

I chaffer English, and I nearly choke, –
O for the talk of simple Russian folk!

The other says: A lonesomeness impels
Me hence; I miss the gossip at the wells ...

I yearn for even Ratno's muds; I long
For the delightfully heart-rending song

Of Reb Yecheskel Chazan, song that tore
The heart so clean it did not ask for more ...

They sigh; they shake their heads; they both conspire
To doom Columbus to eternal fire.

Market Song

Plump pigeons, who will buy?
Plump pigeons, and fat doves?
Come, gossips, hurry nigh;
Shake purses, hearty loves,
   And buy my doves.

Oh, cheap at any price,
A most delicious morsel,
Made ready in a trice!
Take home a feathered parcel,
   A dainty morsel.

Wives, do you love your men?
Set love upon a plate.
A good bird is worth ten
Grown bony in a crate.
   Wives, do not wait!

Go feel them, look at them –
Their breasts, their bright pink eyes!
You buy the like of them
Elsewhere, and at my price,
   My petty price?

Unknot your kerchiefs, then,
Shake out your coins, my loves, –
Buy now, you know not when
You will catch such fat doves,
   Such doves again.

Heirloom

My father bequeathed me no wide estates;
No keys and ledgers were my heritage;
Only some holy books with *yahrzeit* dates
Writ mournfully upon a blank front page –

Books of the Baal Shem Tov, and of his wonders;
Pamphlets upon the devil and his crew;
Prayers against road demons, witches, thunders;
And sundry other tomes for a good Jew.

Beautiful: though no pictures on them, save
The scorpion crawling on a printed track;
The Virgin floating on a scriptural wave,
Square letters twinkling in the Zodiac.

The snuff left on this page, now brown and old,
The tallow stains of midnight liturgy –
These are my coat of arms, and these unfold
My noble lineage, my proud ancestry!

And my tears, too, have stained this heirloomed ground,
When reading in these treatises some weird
Miracle, I turned a leaf and found
A white hair fallen from my father's beard.

Bestiary

God breathe a blessing on
His small bones, every one!
The little boy, who stalks
The Bible's plains and rocks
To hunt in grammar'd woods
Strange litters and wild broods;
The little boy who seeks
Beast-muzzles and bird-beaks
In cave and den and crypt,
In copse of holy script;
The little boy who looks
For quarry in holy books.

Before his eyes is born
The elusive unicorn;
There, scampering, arrive
The golden mice, the five;
Also in antic shape,
Gay peacock and glum ape.
He hears a snort of wrath:
The fiery behemoth!
And then on biblic breeze

The crocodile's sneeze ...
He sees the lion eat
Green stalks ... At tigress-teat,
As if of the same ilk,
The young lamb sucking milk.

Hard by, as fleet as wind,
They pass, the roe and hind.
Bravely, and with no risk,
He halts the basilisk,
Pygarg and cockatrice.
And there, most forest-wise
Among the bestiaries,
The little hunter eyes
Him crawling at his leisure:
The beast Nebuchadnezzar.

Ballad of the Dancing Bear

I

Fat grows Stanislaus, *Pan,* whose
Hamlets teem with busy Jews,

Arguing about one topic:
Thrift of rouble, thrift of kopek;

Tailors, sitting on their shins,
Cutting cloth, and spitting pins;

Bakers kneading their thumbs callous,
Fashioning gigantic *chalos;*

Butchers cutting kosher meat;
Millers raising ghosts of wheat;

Cobbler, praying for bad weather,
Spitting on his polished leather;

Pieman selling children sweets;
Potters hawking in the streets;

Gossips vending Sabbath candles,
Wrapped in paper and in scandals;

Binders gluing holy books,
Liturgies and pentateuchs;

Merchants, or in Slav or jargon,
Driving each his petty bargain.

II

They were rich then, were they not,
With such commerce polygot?

If full moons are yellow cheeses,
If blessed herbs can cure diseases,

If Pan Stanislaus is lean,
Or sheep crafty, or swine clean,

If good words can come from witches,
They, assuredly, had riches!

III

Poor they were, a town of paupers:
Ants rewarded like grasshoppers;

Huts, whose windows storm-abused,
Let in hunger to its roost;

Walls where spider webs were swinging
To the tune of strong winds singing;

Roofs with dried and meagre thatch,
Doors without a knob or latch;

Stool and bed and table broken,
Witness misery outspoken;

And bare pantries where the mice,
Every day starved at least thrice.

IV

For, as all their commerce waxes,
Lo, it wanes beneath hard taxes,

Tax on birth and tax on death,
Tax on gone and coming breath,

Filling Pan Stanislaus' coffers
With the wealth the impost offers,

Keeping him in meats and wines,
Not to speak of concubines,

For the music of gold roubles,
Tintinnabulates his troubles.

Thus, Pan Stanislaus grows fat,
Swilling strong ale from a vat.

V

At the sight of churlish Jew
Thaddeus priest retched forth his spew.

He abhorred the tribe of Moses;
Barbs in his heart were their hooked noses.

So he rummaged the whole Bible,
Seeking some new spicy libel.

Telling beads, he mouthèd curses
That the Lord increase their hearses.

Oh, to sprinkle holy water
On their foul skins – or to slaughter,

Sweep them out like filthy maggots,
Make them crackle on dry faggots,

And as finis to his work,
Ease their whines with fat of pork.

VI

Filaments of evil slip
From the holy spiderlip.

Pan Stanislaus guzzling beer,
Piously inclines his ear:

In our midst there is a people
That thumbs noses at our steeple,

That, though seeming poor, has riches,
Hid in cracks and profane niches,

Stuffed with feathers in their cushions,
Polish coins and German groschens,

And old deeds from peasant-debtors,
Pressed among their sacred letters.

Railing ever at Christ-Jesus,
Every Jew as rich as Croesus, –

Sire, their purses are too heavy;
May your Lordship please to levy

Taxes on the Hebrew scoffers
To replenish Caesar's coffers.

Tax the cradle, tax the coffin;
Jews are never taxed too often.

Therefore, let them be beholden
To their Lord with many a gulden.

Let the folk whose life besmirches
Us, erect our ruined churches.

So, while each Jew weeps his dirge, he
Helps to feed God's favourite clergy.

Be it that they will not pay,
Let them further on their way,

Bearing on unbaptized legs,
All their holy thingumjigs.

Pan Stanislaus yawned, and drank,
Drank and yawned, his vile mouth stank;

Ho, he said, and *hum*, he said,
Scratched his fumed and dizzying head,

Wiped back each mustachio,
And then hiccupped: Be it so.

VII

When the crier cried the news
To the hamletful of Jews,

They were nibbling each his crumb,
They were smitten dumb.

But they donned no sackcloth, for
Sackcloth were the clothes they wore.

They poured ashes on their heads;
Fasted; they ate Sorrow's breads.

And to live through these grim threats,
They bribed God with epithets.

VIII

In the castle-tower, she
Sings her sorrow wistfully,

Paulinka, the princess, sings
Valiant but uncouth things:

Giants slain by manikins;
Beanstalks climbed by crippled shins;

Ogres discomfited by maimed
Knights that in an hour are famed;

Lions bearded in their dens
By an outcast pauper-prince;

Hunchback troubadours who wed
Princesses of royal blood;

Kingdoms in remote lands won
By a disinherited son;

Imps in pandemonium
Cowering before Tom Thumb.

In the tower alone, she sings
Of God's ill unfavoured things.

Paulinka forgets her maim
Singing; she, alas, is lame.

From her couch she sadly watches
Days that amble by on crutches.

Old wives say it was a witch,
Sired of demon, dam'd of bitch,

Cursed her with an evil spell,
(May she shrivel up in hell).

Pan Stanislaus sent for sages;
Tartar quacks and eastern mages,

Doctors bearing bitter potions,
Broths and brews and mystic lotions;

Monk and priest and sorcerer,
All came kneeling unto her.

Vain the prayers; frustrate the brews;
The incantation of small use;

Fickle the astrolabe; the wise
Mutter, yet she can not rise.

Upon her couch she sits and sings
Of the Lord's unfavoured things.

IX

Lustier was the village dog
Than the Jews in the synagogue.

All were sore perplexed, save Motka,
Blithe as if he had drunk vodka,

And not carried on his shoulders
Water-pails as large as boulders.

His eyes were like dots of flame,
The iotas of God's name.

Flourishes on holy script:
Hairs with which his chin was tipped.

On his brow the *tfillin* set
Seemed a Hebrew coronet.

Tzizith danced against his legs,
Jubilant with caftan-rags.

It was rumoured he was one
For whom God preserved the sun.

Thus in some way, rather subtle,
It was manifest to Mottel

That the Lord could not reject,
Nay, nor scorn His Hebrew sect.

X

Jews do now prepare to wend
Their long way to the world's end.

Hope grows great, like three-day yeast,
In the heart of Thaddeus priest.

Motka peddles joy; no worries
Come to mar his witty stories.

In the castle-tower, the
Princess sings most wistfully.

Stanislaus the baron nuzzles
Foaming beer-mugs; as he guzzles

A thought pierces through his skull,
A thought torturesomely droll:

'Bring me to my banquet-table,
Come this night, a Hebrew able

To hop sprightly, to amuse
Stanislaus well rid of Jews.'

XI

Jews, cease lamentation; throttle
Sorrow; I will dance, says Mottel.

Lords and barons, dukes and pans,
Seated on their silk divans,

At the banquet-feast prepare
To see Motka dance in air.

Barons slap their Christian thighs
As they see tall Motka rise,

Dancing, waving paws in air,
A pathetic Hebrew bear,

Flaunting his ungrizzly beard,
Ignorant of knaves who jeered.

A huge moujik cracks his whip
Loudly to make Mottel skip.

The bear leaps, he hops, he prances,
Tzizith flutter as he dances.

Drummers, drum! and fiddlers, fiddle!
Make a music for the Zhid'l!

Happy as a bloated louse,
The fat baron Stanislaus

Swills his beer, and munches pork
While he keeps time with his fork.

Motka leaps, he pirouettes,
Gasps and gambols, Motka sweats.

With God's praises on his lips
Motka capersomely skips.

Barons pat their shaking paunches,
Motka rises on his haunches,

Leaps and dances; when behold!
By his rhythms so cajoled,

Even servants drop their plates,
Drop the ducal delicates;

Guardian-varlets leave their stances
And leap into Mottel's dances.

Yea, the butler breaks his bottle
As he strives to out-do Mottel.

Lo! the Pan, sucking a bone,
Suddenly forsakes his throne,

With him in the circle hop
All the lords; they cannot stop.

Drummers, drum! and fiddlers, fiddle!
Make a music for the Zhid'l!

For from off her couch she rises,
Paulinka the princess, rises,

No more a bed-ridden cripple, –
Tall, her lovely limbs most supple,

Rises, trips toward him, halts,
And takes Motka for a waltz!

XII

In the hamlet busy Jews
Ply their trades in wonted use.

Thaddeus priest now tells his beads,
While his stone heart bleeds, and bleeds.

Paulinka the princess sings
Of God's unforsaken things.

In Pan Stanislaus's throat
Overbrimming bumpers float.

Motka sells his crystal waters,
Earning dowries for his daughters.

And God in His heaven hums,
Twiddling His contented thumbs.

Baal Shem Tov

Be his memory forever green and rich,
Like moss upon a stone at a brook's edge,
That rabbi of infants, man of children's love,
Greybeard and leader of tots, the Baal Shem Tov!
Who hearing a child's song float on sunlit air
Heard far more piety than in a prayer
That issued from ten synagogal throats;
Who seeing an urchin bring a starved mare oats,
Beheld that godliness which can break bars
Of heaven padlocked with its studded stars;
The Baal Shem Tov, who better than liturgy
Loved speech with teamsters and with gypsies! Be
His memory ever splendid like a jewel,
His, who bore children on his back to school
And with a trick to silence their small grief
Crossed many a stream upon a handkerchief.
Oh, be there ever pure minds and bright eyes,
Homage of children ever, eulogies
Of little folk so that the humble fame
Of the Baal Shem, the Master of the Name,
May be forever green and fresh and rich
Like moss upon a stone at a brook's edge.

Elijah

Elijah in a long beard
With a little staff
Hobbles through the market
And makes the children laugh.

He crows like a rooster,
He dances like a bear,
While the long-faced rabbis
Drop their jaws to stare.

He tosses his skullcap
To urchin and tot,
And catches it neatly
Right on his bald spot.

And he can tell stories
Of lovers who elope;
And terrible adventures
With cardinal and pope.

Without a single pinch, and
Without a blow or cuff,
We learned from him the Aleph,
We learned from him the Tauph.

Between the benedictions
We would play leapfrog –
O, this was a wonderful
Synagogue!

He can make a whistle
From a gander's quill;
He can make a mountain
Out of a molehill.

Oh, he is a great man!
Wished he, he could whoop
The moon down from heaven,
And roll it like a hoop;

Wished he, he could gather
The stars from the skies,
And juggle them like marbles
Before our very eyes.

Scholar

A goat a scholar,
A goat a sage,
That ate *gemara*
From a grassy page!

Hot for wisdom
His dry mouth lipped
The small green mosses, –
His *rashi* script.

For higher lore
He chewed red clover;
He conned his Torah
Over and over.

And when his throat
Went dry on this book,
He ran and drank from
A garrulous brook.

Then up on his two
Hind legs stood he

And scratched his horns
Against a tree.

And crooned a *mishna*
In a voice most weird,
And nodded his wise pate,
And shook his beard.

Upon my word,
A learned one!
A scholar out of
Babylon!

The Venerable Bee

The *shamash* of the glade,
The venerable bee,
In caftan bright arrayed,
Hums honeyed liturgy.

He brushes off the dust
From sacred leaves; he frees
With but a single thrust
The arks of chalices.

The convoluted rose
Is *torah* scroll to him:
He reads, with index-nose,
Of bee-like seraphim.

Tendril and bud he sees
To signify God's yoke
In green phylacteries
For all his kindred folk.

Gay fields and flowered walks,
His many-coloured home,
Will scent his *besomim* box,
His fragrant honeycomb.

Blessed is that happy one,
Who from a sylvan pew
Attends his *kiddush* on
A flowercup of dew.

Rev Owl

Erudite, solemn,
The pious bird
Sits on a tree,
His *shtreimel* furred.

The owl, chief rabbi
Of the woods,
In moonlight ponders
Worldly goods.

With many a legal
To who? To wit?
He nightly parses
Holy writ.

And then tears gizzards
Of captured fowl
To find them kosher
For an owl.

Orders

Muffle the wind;
Silence the clock;
Muzzle the mice;
Curb the small talk;
Cure the hinge-squeak;
Banish the thunder.
Let me sit silent,
Let me wonder.

Diary of Abraham Segal, Poet

7:15. – He Rises.

No cock rings matins of the dawn for me;
No morn, in russet mantle clad,
Reddens my window-pane; no melodye
Maken the smalle fowles nigh my bed.
The lark at heaven's gate may sing, may sing,
And Phoebus may arise;
And little birds make a sweet jargoning;
And shepherds pipe their pastoral minstrelsies;
All these things well may be; my slug-a-bed ears
Hear them not; nor see them my bronze eyes.

No triple braggadocio of the cock,
But the alarum of a dollar clock,
Ten sonorous riveters at heaven's gate;
Steel udders rattled by milkmen; horns
Cheerily rouse me on my Monday morns.

Is it a wonder then, that in my dreams,
My five o'clock dreams, my boon-companions are
Ogres in planes, ranunculi in ships,
Thin witches mounting escalators, imps
Hopping from telephones, and negresses
Lipping spirituals into radios?
Is it a wonder that these cauchemars stamp
With elves on girders i' the light of the moon,
Or with wild worshippers before a mazda lamp?

So have
They clipped the wings
Of fiery seraphim,
And made of them, – ye angels, weep! –
Dusters ...

*8:15. – He Travels on the Street-Car, and Reads over a
Neighbour's Shoulder.*

Communists ask for more bank holidays.
A broken heart is glued by so much. Ex-
Champion scores k.o. on his wife. No sex
Appeal, say critics of two bankrupt plays.
Actress weds crown-prince. Zulu bob new craze.
Bootleg kills ten. Tenor smokes only Rex.
Girl dances hula robed in cancelled cheques.
Convicted murderess weeps: The woman pays.
Champagne bath brings eczema. New gang wars
Disturb police. Explorer still alive.
xy declares yx controls chain stores.
Screen star makes seventh matrimonial dive.
Upholster Spanish throne. Man seeks divorce
Because his wife (continued on page five).

8:45. – He Considers the Factory Hands.

What a piece of work is man! the paragon
Of animals! the beauty of the world!
So Dr. Aesculapius Pavlov
Dissects cadavers, and reports as follows:
Fats in this human paragon, enough
For so much soap; for so much writing, lead;
Two thousand match-heads from his phosphorus;
A nail from his iron, medium-sized head;
Magnesium – one full-sized powder, plus;
Whitewash enough for one coop, board and crack;
Sufficient arsenic to leave them dead,
The fleas upon a bitch's front and back;
In fine, each worth a dollar, dames or gents, –
In U.S. money, eighty-seven cents.

9:05. – He Yawns; and Regards the Slogans on the Office Walls.

Blessed the men this day,
Whether at death or birth,
Who own good sites, for they
Shall inherit the earth.

The Lord in silence works
Towards mysterious ends.
The same omniscience lurks
In dividends.

Open, ye gates, before
The man who gets or gives!
Open, thrice-padlocked door, –
Executives!

Scorn not the profiteer,
Minor or major; priest,

Bard, speculative seer,
Moneytheist.

Initiative – this was,
Is, and will be our foil.
Consider the bloom which does
Not spin, nor toil.

In sacred stocks, O Lord,
Impound us; bind our wounds
For sweet sake of Thy word,
In hallowed bonds!

11:30. – He Receives a Visitor.

Milady Schwartz, beloved of the boss,
Married with documents, parturitive,
Into the office waddles, makes a pause
To note the pimply girls, her choice, still live;
Then sweetly coos to hubby dearest, pats
The proud oasis of his glabrous head,
And with her pendulous chins, and gold teeth, smiles
Amorously at the giver of her bread.
He is too busy signing cheques, post-dated.
Milady Schwartz, (oh, no, she is no snob)
Speaks to the staff: The season is belated.
Her husband works too hard. You'd never think
So fine a soul would take to cloaks and suits,
Competing with such thieves as Levy, Inc.
But she does not complain. We all must suffer
For these the higher things life has to offer.
Does Mr. Abram Segal still write verses?
It must be wonderful. She envies him.
She wishes she could make up rhymes. She nurses
Feelings unuttered, smitten by lockjaw.
(Moi, j'ai Apollon sur les bouts de mes dix doigts ...)
Of course she just loves art. She goes to lectures.

But yesterday she heard a recitation
About the patter of a babe's pink toes.
He should have heard it, should the poet Abe.
Also, she is a member of a club
Occasionally addressed by local bards.
(A teaspoonful of art, before and after cards.)
Milady Schwartz, aware she is confiding
Beyond the limits of her dignity;
She must not talk so much about herself.
Are we all happy at our several jobs?
Wages are low, but hope eternal bobs
Upwards; and money, after all, is pelf.
Moreover, so many poor people go
Looking for work, tramping their both legs lame,
It is a pity, a disgrace, a shame!
Why only last week she was overjoyed
To go to the Grand Ball, Chez Madame Lloyd,
And dance all night for the poor unemployed.
Milady Schwartz utters her shrill goodbyes,
Lets love domestic issue from her eyes,
And from her plump hand, jewelled with costly warts,
Wafts kisses. Exit Lady Schwartz.

12:20. – He Worships at the North-Eastern.

In one-armed restaurants where Cretan floors
Mosaically crawl towards Alpine walls,
The human soul, like a brave leopard, roars,
Like a young lion, *de profundis*, calls:
Waiter, a plate of beans.
Waiter, some coffee and toast.
Waiter, inform the Lord, our Host.
Snappy, I says what I means!

From behind the marble lichen
Providence thunders: Clean the kitchen ...
The customer pays the pale cashier.

The Angel punches the register:
    A soul ate here.

12:20–12:45. – He Reads His Pocket-Edition of Shakespeare; and Luxuriously Thinks.

Beneath this fretted roof, the knave, swag-bellied,
Struts him before his calibans i' the sun,
Gloats o'er his shillings, byzants, ducats, smiles
At gaunt clerks, their nockandros flat on stools,
With borrowed quills in hired tomes accounting
His profit, his sweet profit, sweet sweet profit.

The villain smiles: if fools be fools, why, let them,
If sweat on their lips is nectar, here's a health!
They wake to toil? They sleep to dream of toiling?
Be their days long upon this earth.

Aye, but these have immortal yearnings. So.
The brimstone brabble of divines looks to't,
Granting the widow her fond spouse in heaven,
The maimed celestial wings, the dumb a harp,
The starved, ethereal guts ... But mark, these dudgeons,
Even these blocks, these stones, these honoured men,
Quick at such pleasures metaphysical,
Seeking the grosser lust, the grander passion,
They clink their canakins in pot-houses,
And swollen with wine, they mouth brave oaths, and cry, –
Out with your fee-fi-fum of ichor blood!
A fico for your flibbertigibbet god!
Then staggering in dark lanes, their bodkins raised,
They hail a perfumed placket, and drool, 'Chuck,
Let me lie in thy lap, Ophelia.'

6:30. – He Eats at the Family-Board.

Because to Him in prayershawl, he prays,
My father's God absolves his cares and carks;
My wedded sister likes no empty phrase,
Her spaniel brings her cash, not learned barks.
My brother in his bed-room den displays
The dark capacious beard of Herr Karl Marx;
My uncle scorns them all; my uncle says
Herzl will turn the Jews, now moles, to larks;
My cousin, amiable, believes them both,
Serving a beard of Herzlian-Marxian growth.

And as for me, unlike the ancient bards,
My idols have been shattered into shards.

7:15. – He Contemplates His Contemporaries.

La chair est triste, hélas, et j'ai lu tous les livres.
An octopus of many tentacles,
Boredom, enjoins the slow heart, the dead pulse,
With north as drab as south, and south as dull
As the gray east, the west unbeautiful,
Where shall I go? What pathway shall I choose?
Where shall I point the nozzles of my shoes?
Around the corner is a cinema,
Where heroines squeak, 'Oh,' and knaves gasp 'Ah ...'
Where paupers get their feet numb, buttocks callous,
Watching wealth serve a grand vicarious phallus.
Therefore, my soul, not there! A pool-room? No.
A dance-hall? No. A lecturer? No! no!
My friends? My bitter friends, at loggerheads,
The blackshirts, the bluestockings, and the reds,
Evoke from me the vast abysmal yawn:
The poet, with the unmowed cranial lawn
(And Shakespeare, he was bald! ...) the theolog
Anent the sure uncleanliness of hog;

The dandy, boasting of his latest moll;
The lawyer, and his case; the radical
Pounding upon an unprovisioned table
Rendering it, not Canada, unstable –
All, in the end, despite their savage feuds, –
Italic voices uttering platitudes.

So Segal, undernourished, surfeited,
Wearied but sleepless, sick at heart, abashed,
Giving his anguish voice, cries: Life is dead
Echo, and letters – macaronics washed
From distant shores upon a rocky bed ...

9:00. – He Communes with Nature.

Within the meadow on the mountain-top
Abe Segal and his sweetheart, lie. Lover,
Sweet is the comradeship of grass, the crop
Being mown, the hay dry, dry the clover;
And sweet the fiddling of the crickets, dear
The bird-song for a prothalamium.
They see again, his eyes which once were blear.
His heart gets speech, and is no longer dumb.

Before the glass o' the moon, no longer high,
Abe Segal nattily adjusts his tie.
Gone the insistence of inveterate clocks;
The heart at last can flutter from its bars.
Upon the mountain top, Abe Segal walks,
Hums old-time songs, of old-time poets talks,
Brilliant his shoes with dew, his hair with stars ...

from 'Of Castles in Spain'

Sonnet without Music

Upon the piazza, haemophilic dons
delicately lift their sherry in the sun.

Having recovered confiscated land,
and his expropriated smile redeemed,
the magnate, too, has doff'd his socialized face.
He beams a jocund aftermath to bombs.

Also, the priest, – alas, for so much bloodshed! –
cups plumpish hand to catch uncatechized belch.

The iron heel grows rusty in the nape
of peasant feeding with the earthworm – but
beware aristocrat, Don Pelph, beware!
The peon soon will stir, will rise, will stand,
breathe Hunger's foetid breath, lift arm, clench fist,
and heil you to the fascist realm of death!

from 'Barricade Smith: His Speeches'

I

Of Violence

What does the word mean: *Violence?*
                                  Are we not content?
Do not our coupons fall, like manna, from the bonds?

Are we not all well-fed?
                              Save for twelve months of Lent?
Is it not slander to aver the Boss absconds
With all the embezzled dollars in his delicate hand?
Is there not heard a sound
Of belching in the land?

Who, then, would speak of violence, uncouth and impolite?
Surely not we, the meek, the docile, the none-too-bright!
The askers with cap-in-hand, the rebels, à Emily Post
Who know too well our place, our manners,
                                        and our host!

Wherefore, though wages slither, and upward soar the rates,
Not we will be the churls rudely to doubt that boast
Of Labor and Capital, that Siamese twin alright,
One of whom eats, the other defecates.

The Board of Directors sits
And cudgels its salaried wits: –
At cost of life and limb
Show profits, and still be
Unviolent as a hymn.

They syncopate your groans
                    on gramaphones;
Your muscles throb in their Rolls-Royce;
They triturate your sweat in cocktail-shakers.

But they are not violent, for violence is wicked;
And worse than that – I shudder to say the word,
That fell indictment –
It simply is not cricket!

Go therefore, tell your wives that the breadbox must stay
   breadless,

The rent unpaid, the stove unheated, you enslaved;
Because you *must* be above *all* things, well-behaved.
And having uttered these heroic words, slink hence
Into some unleased corner, and there vanish –
But not with any violence.

II

Of Dawn and Its Breaking

Where will you be
When the password is said and the news is extra'd abroad,
And the placard is raised, and the billboard lifted on high,
And the radio network announces its improvised decree:
You are free?
Where will it find you, that great genesis?
Preparing your lips for a kiss?
Waiting the call of next in a barbershop?
Rapt with the ticker's euphony?
Or practising some negroid hop?
Where will you be
When the news is bruited by the auto horn?
Holding a pair of aces back to back?
Paring a toe-nail, cutting out a corn?
Or reading, with de-trousered back,
Hearst's tabloid, previously torn?

Or will you be – O would that you should be! –
Among those valiant ones returning to their homes
                                    To tell
Their daughters and their sons to tell posterity
How they did on that day,
If not create new heaven, at least abolish hell.

IV

Of Psalmody in the Temple

They do lie heavily upon me, these
Sores of the spirit, failings of the flesh!
Wherefore, O triply-purgatoried soul,
Scram;
And chastened O my body,
Take it on the lam –
To the colossal, suprasuper hideout, blow,
To the lotiferous movie-show!

There I do sit me down in thick upholstery;
I do not want.
A tale is prepared before me: heroine enters,
Slim; and a villain, gaunt:
Also a well-groomed esquire saying *I love you* –
Fade out, fade in;
Shots of a lot of legs, and a couple of stooges,
Close-up, a grin.
The decent, the fair, win prizes; the wicked
Their just deserts.
The prince weds Cinderella, and virtue triumphs
Until it hurts.

O these felicitous endings, sweet finales,
They comfort me –
O bodies' beatitude, O soul's salvation,
Where this can be!
Most surely I shall dwell in this great temple
And take my bliss
Forever out of scenes which end forever
In an eight-foot kiss.

VI

Of Beauty

Seeing that planets move by dynamos,
And even the sun's a burnished well-oiled spring,
What glory is there, say, in being a rose
And why should skylarks still desire to sing,
Singing, and no men hear, men standing close
Over some sleek, mechanic and vociferous thing?

For these there is one beauty; put it on a table:
A loaf of bread, some salt, a vegetable.

In Re Solomon Warshawer

On Wodin's day, sixth of December, thirty-nine,
I, Friedrich Vercingetorix, attached
to the VIIth Eavesdroppers-behind-the-Line,
did cover my beat, when, suddenly, the crowd I watched
surrounded, in a cobbled lane one can't pass through,
a bearded man, in rags disguised, a Jew.

In the said crowd there were a number of Poles.
Mainly, however, there were Germans there:
blood-brothers of our Reich, true Aryan souls,
breathing at last – in Warsaw – Nordic air.
These were the words the Jew was shouting:
I took them down verbatim:

Whom have I hurt? Against whose silk have I brushed?
On which of your women looked too long?
I tell you I have done no wrong!
Send home your children, lifting hardened dung,

And let your curs be hushed!
For I am but beard and breathlessness, and chased enough.
Leave me in peace, and let me go my way.

At this the good folk laughed. The Jew continued to say
he was no thief; he was a man for hire;
worked for his bread, artist or artisan;
a scribe, if you wished; a vendor; even buyer;
work of all kinds, and anything at all:
paint a mural, scour a latrine,
indite an ode, repair an old machine,
anything, to repeat,
anything at all,
so that he might eat
and have his pallet in his abandoned stall.

Asked for his papers, he made a great to-do
of going through the holes in his rags, whence he withdrew
a Hebrew pamphlet and a signet ring,
herewith produced, Exhibits 1 and 2.

I said: No documents in a civilized tongue?
He replied:

Produce, O Lord, my wretched fingerprint,
Bring forth, O angel in the heavenly court,
My dossier, full, detailed, both fact and hint,
Felony, misdemeanor, tort!

I refused to be impressed by talk of that sort.

From further cross-examination, it appeared,
immediate history: a beggar in Berlin;
chased, as a vagrant, from the streets of Prague;
kept, as a leper, in forced quarantine;
shunned as the pest, avoided like the plague;
then had escaped, mysteriously come

by devious routes and stolen frontiers to
the *nalewkas* of Warsaw's sheenydom.

Pressed to reveal his true identity,
he lied:

One of the anthropophagi was he,
or, if we wished, a denizen of Mars,
the ghost of *my* father, Conscience – aye,
the anatomy of Reason, naked, and with scars;
even became insulting, said he was
Aesop the slave among the animals ...
Sir Incognito ... Rabbi Alias ...
The eldest elder of Zion ... said we knew
his numerous varied oriental shapes,
even as we ought to know his present guise –
the man in the jungle, and beset by apes.

It was at this point the S.S. man arrived.
The Jew was interrupted. When he was revived,
he deposed as follows:

At low estate, a beggar, and in flight,
Still do I wear my pride like purple. I
Do fear you, yes, but founder not from fright.
Already I breathe your unfuturity.
For you are not the first whom I have met –
O I have known them all,
The dwarf dictators, the diminutive dukes,
The heads of straw, the hearts of gall,
Th' imperial plumes of eagles covering rooks!

It is not necessary to name names,
But it may serve anon,
Now to evoke from darkness some dark fames,
Evoke,
Armada'd Spain, that gilded jettison;
And Russia's last descended Romanov,

Descending a dark staircase
To a dank cellar at Ekaterinoslov;
Evoke
The peacock moulted from the Persian loom ...
Babylon tumbled from its terraces ...
Decrescent and debased Mizraim, remembered only
By that one star that sentries Pharaoh's tomb ...
Evoke
O Greece! O broken marble! ...
And disinterred unresurrected Rome ...

They would have harried me extinct, these thrones!
Set me, archaic, in their heraldries,
Blazon antique! ... For they were Powers ... Once! ...
But I, though still exilian, rest extant,
And on my cicatrices tally off
Their undone dynasties!
Shall I dread you – who overlived all these?

Here impudence was duly rebuked, and the Jew
confronted with Exhibit 2.

Yes, but that signet ring! ... Freiherr, that seal
Once flashed the pleasure majestatical!
For I, who in tatters stand investitured,
Who, to these knightly men, am dislodged pawn,
Abdicate and abjured,
I was, I am, the Emperor Solomon!
O, to and fro upon the face of the earth,
I wandered, crying: Ani Shlomo, but –
But no one believed my birth.

For he now governs in my place and stead,
He who did fling me from Jerusalem
Four hundred parasangs!
Who stole the crown from off my head!
Who robed him in my robes! Beneath whose hem

The feet of the cock extend, the tail of the demon hangs!
Asmodeus!

Mistake me not; I am no virtuous saint;
Only a man, and like all men, not god-like ...
From birth beset by his own heart's constraint,
Its brimstone pride, the cinders of its greed,
(Brazier behind the ribs that will not faint!)
Beset, inflamed, besooted, charred, indeed, –
Only a man, and like all men, not god-like,
Damned by desire –
But I at least fought down that bellows'd gleed,
Tried to put out the sulphurs of that fire! ...
At least craved wisdom, how to snuff the blaze,
Sought knowledge, to unravel good from evil,
Sought guidance from the Author of my Days.

The understanding heart, and its enthymemes,
Being granted me, I learned from beast ... bird ... man;
Would know; and eavesdropped nest ... and house ... and lair.
The wild beasts spoke to me, told me their dreams,
Which, always biped, towards the human ran ...
O, how that flesh did long to doff its fur!
The fluttering birds, the twittering birds of the air:
'Would you cast off from your feet,' they said, 'earth's mass,
That weighted globe of brass,
And soar into your own?
With azure fill your heart! ... Be hollow of bone!'
And from my self, and from the breed of Adam,
I fathom'd that heart's depths, how it may sink
Down to the deep and ink of genesis,
And lie there, that once could the heavens explore,
A sponge and pulse of hunger on the ocean-floor ...
Saw also, and praised, for then knew possible,
The heart's saltations! ...
That always – vanitatum vanitas! –
That always after back to grossness fell.

Thus taught, thus prompted, upward I essay'd, —
Some not mean triumphs scored,
Spread truth, spread song, spread justice, which prevailed,
Builded that famous footstool for the Lord, —
Yet human, human among mortals, failed!
Was thwarted the greater yearning, the jubilee
Wherein the race might at the last be hailed
Transcendent of its own humanity!
For I Qoheleth, King in Jerusalem,
Ecclesiast of the troubled apothegm,
Concluding the matter, must affirm mankind
Still undivined.

However, though worsted, I had wrestled, but he —

Our royal Jew, now questioned *in camera*,
was not, this time, molested. It was thought
some enemy intelligence might come through
from his distractions, some inkling of the plot
now being pursued by his ten losing tribes.
Therefore the record, as ordered, here gives the whole Jew, —
for which the subscribing officer subscribes
apology.

But he, unspeakable prince of malice!
Usurper of my throne, pretender to the Lord's!
Wicked, demoniac, lycanthropous,
Goad of the succubi, horrific hordes!
Master of the worm, pernicious, that cleaves rocks,
The beast that talks,
Asmodeus!

Who has not felt his statutes? ... His scientists,
Mastering for him the lethal mysteries;
His surgeons of doctrine, cutting, like vile cysts
From off the heart, all pities and sympathies;
His judges, trembling over their decrees,

Lest insufficient injustice displease;
And his psychiaters, guarding against relapse,
For fear the beast, within the man, collapse.

His statecraft, and its modes and offices?
Here motive is appetite; and oestric hate
The force that freaks and fathers all device.
All love's venereal; or excess; or bait.
Ambush all policy, and artifice;
And all reward conferred, all honour
Hierarchical to the degrees of Hate.

Upon his lych-throne, robed in bloodied purple,
Listening to those harmonies where the sigh
Exhaling greets the groan, the groan is pitched to the cry,
Asmodeus sits;
And I –

At this point the S.S. men departed.
The Jew was not revived. He was carried and carted,
and to his present gaoler brought;
awaiting higher pleasure.
                    And further deponent saith not.

A Psalm of Abraham, When He Hearkened to a Voice, and There Was None

Since prophecy has vanished out of Israel,
And since the open vision is no more,
Neither a word on the high places, nor the Urim and Thummim,
Nor even a witch, foretelling, at En-dor, –
Where in these dubious days shall I take counsel?
Who is there to resolve the dark, the doubt?

O, these are the days of scorpions and of whips
When all the seers have had their eyes put out,
And all the prophets burned upon the lips!

There is noise only in the groves of Baal.
Only the painted heathen dance and sing,
With frenzied clamouring.
Among the holy ones, however, is no sound at all.

A Psalm of Abraham, When He Was Sore Pressed

Would that the Lord had made me, in place of man-child, beast!
Even an ox of the field, content on grass,
On clover and cud content, had made me, made me the least
Of his creatures, one of a herd, to pass
As cattle, pastured and driven and sold and bought
To toil on ploughland or before a cart!
For easier is the yoke than the weight of thought,
Lighter the harness than the harnessed heart!

A Prayer of the Afflicted, When He Is Overwhelmed

I would not tell this to the man met on the street,
The casual acquaintance, even the intimate friend,
Stopping to speak of the news, complain about the heat:
Him would I tell my triumphs mount, and have no end,
And tricks are fine, thank you, and never were they better.
But to tell you, O Lord, it is a different matter –
I would not have you pity my cheap lies.
You know the truth, the ache I have and had,

The blind alleys, the frustrations, and the sighs.
O Lord, the times they are not good at all,
And one might even say that they are bad.

A Psalm of Abraham, concerning That Which He Beheld upon the Heavenly Scarp

1
And on that day, upon the heavenly scarp,
The hosannahs ceased, the hallelujahs died,
And music trembled on the silenced harp.
An angel, doffing his seraphic pride,
Wept; and his tears so bitter were, and sharp,
That where they fell, the blossoms shrivelled and died.

2
Another with such voice intoned his psalm
It sang forth blasphemy against the Lord.
Oh, that was a very imp in angeldom,
Who, thinking evil, said no evil word –
But only pointed, at each *Te Deum*
Down to the earth, and its abhorrèd horde.

3
The Lord looked down, and saw the cattle-cars:
Men ululating to a frozen land.
He saw a man tear at his flogged scars,
And saw a babe look for its blown-off hand.
Scholars, he saw, sniffing their bottled wars,
And doctors who had geniuses unmanned.

4
The gentle violinist whose fingers played
Such godly music, washing a gutter, with lye,

He saw. He heard the priest who called His aid.
He heard the agnostic's undirected cry.
Unto Him came the odour Hunger made,
And the odour of blood before it is quite dry.

5
The angel who wept looked into the eyes of God.
The angel who sang ceased pointing to the earth.
A little cherub, now glimpsing God's work flaw'd,
Went mad, and flapped his wings in crazy mirth.
And the good Lord said nothing, but with a nod
Summoned the angels of Sodom down to earth.

Grace before Poison

Well may they thank thee, Lord, for drink and food:
For daily benison of meat,
For fish or fowl,
For spices of the subtle cook,
For fruit of the orchard, root of the meadow, berry of the wood;
For all things good,
And for the grace of water of the running brook!
And in the hallelujah of these joys
Not least is my uplifted voice.

But this day into thy great temple have I come
To praise thee for the poisons thou has brayed,
To thank thee for pollens venomous, the fatal gum,
The banes that bless, the multifarious herbs arrayed
In all the potency of that first week
Thou didst compose the sextet of Earth spoken, made!

Behold them everywhere, the unuttered syllables of thy breath,
Heavy with life, and big with death!
The flowering codicils to thy great fiat!

The hemp of India – and paradise!
The monk's hood, cooling against fever;
And nightshade: death unpetalled before widened eyes;
And blossom of the heart, the purple foxglove!
The spotted hemlock, punishment and prize,
And those exhilarators of the brain:
Cocaine;
Blood of the grape; and marrow of the grain!

And sweet white flower of thy breath, O Lord,
Juice of the poppy, conjuror of timeless twilights,
Eternities of peace in which the fretful world
Like a tame tiger at the feet lies curled.

To the Chief Musician, Who Played for the Dancers

These were the ones who thanked their God
With dancing jubilant shins:
The beggar, who for figleaf pride
Sold shoelaces and pins;
The blindman for his brotherly dog;
The cripple for his chair;
The mauled one for the blessed gasp
Of the cone of sweet kind air.
I did not see this dance, but men
Have praised its grace; yet I
Still cannot fathom how they danced,
Or why.

A Prayer of Abraham, against Madness

Lord, for the days allotted me,
Preserve me whole, preserve me hale!
Spare me the scourge of surgery.
Let not my blood nor members fail.

But if Thy will is otherwise,
And I am chosen such an one
For maiming and for maladies –
So be it; and Thy will be done.

Palsy the keepers of the house;
And of the strongmen take Thy toll.
Break down the twigs; break down the boughs.
But touch not, Lord, the golden bowl!

O, I have seen these touched ones –
Their fallow looks, their barren eyes –
For whom have perished all the suns
And vanished all fertilities;

Who, docile, sit within their cells
Like weeds, within a stagnant pool.
I have seen also their fierce hells,
Their flight from echo, their fight with ghoul.

Behold him scrabbling on the door!
His spittle falls upon his beard,
As, cowering, he whines before
The voices and the visions, feared.

Not these can serve Thee. Lord, if such
The stumbling that awaits my path –
Grant me Thy grace, Thy mortal touch,
The full death-quiver of Thy wrath!

A Psalm of Abraham of That Which Was Visited upon Him

A prowler in the mansion of my blood!
I have not seen him, but I know his signs.
Sometimes I hear him meddling with my food,
Or in the cellar, poisoning my wines, —

Yet face to face with him I never come;
But by a foot print, by a book misplaced,
Or by the imprint of an inky thumb,
Or by the next day's meal, a strange new taste,

I know that he has breached my household peace,
I know that somehow he has let him in.
Shall I fling open a window, and shout *Police!*
I dare not. He is of my kith and kin.

A Psalm to Teach Humility

O sign and wonder of the barnyard, more
beautiful than the pheasant, more melodious
than nightingale! O creature marvellous!

Prophet of sunrise, and foreteller of times!
Vizier of the constellations! Sage,
red-bearded, scarlet-turbaned, in whose brain
the stars lie scattered like well-scattered grain!

Calligraphist upon the barnyard page!
Five-noted balladist! Crower of rhymes!

O morning-glory mouth, O throat of dew,
announcing the out-faring of the blue,
the greying and the going of the night,
the coming on,
the imminent coming of the dawn,
the coming of the kinsman, the brightly-plumaged sun!

O creature marvellous – and O blessed Creator,
Who givest to the rooster wit
to know the movements of the turning day,
to understand, to herald it,
better than I, who neither sing nor crow
and of the sun's goings and comings nothing know.

A Psalm or Prayer – Praying His Portion with Beasts

The better to understand Thy ways,
Divinity I would divine,
Let me companion all my days
The more-than-human beasts of Thine;

The sheep whose little woolly throat
Taught the child Isaac sacrifice;
The dove returning to Noah's boat,
Sprigless, and with tearful eyes;

The ass instructing Balaam
The discourse of inspired minds;
And David's lost and bleating lamb,
And Solomon's fleet lovely hinds;

Enfold me in their fold, and let
Me learn their mystic parables –

Of food that desert ravens set,
And of the lion's honeyed fells.

Above all, teach me blessedness
Of him, Azazel, that dear goat,
Sent forth into the wilderness
To hallow it with one sad note.

A Psalm of Abraham, to Be Written Down and Left on the Tomb of Rashi

Now, in this terrible tumultuous night,
When roars the metal beast, the steel bird screams,
And images of God, for fraud or fright,
Cannot discern what is from that which seems, —
I, in bewilderment, remember you,
Mild pedagogue, who took me, young and raw,
And led me, verse by verse, and clue by clue,
Mounting the spiral splendid staircase of the Law, —
You, Rabbi Solomon bar Isaac, known
Rashi, incomparable exegete,
Who did sustain my body and my bone
With drink talmudic and with biblic meat, —
Simple, and for a child were they, your words,
Bringing into the silent wooded script,
Texts that came twittering, like learned birds,
Describing mightily the nondescript.
Not these can I forget, nor him ignore,
That old archaic Frank expounding lore
From his Hebraic crypt.

Nothing was difficult, O Master, then,
No query but it had an answer, clear, —

But now though I am grown, a man of men,
The books all read, the places seen, the dear
Too personal heart endured all things, there is
Much that I cannot grasp, and much that goes amiss,
And much that is a mystery that even the old Gaul,
Nor Onkelus, nor Jonathan, can lucidate at all.

Yours were such days, great rabbi, like these days,
When blood was spilled upon the public ways,
And lives were stifled, for mere glut of gore,
As they marched on, those murderous four,
Hunger and hate and pestilence and war!
   Wherefore, O Parshandatha of the law,
Unriddle me the chapter of the week:
Show me the wing, the hand, behind the claw,
The human mouth behind the vulture beak;
Reveal, I pray you, do reveal to me
Behind the veil the vital verity;
Show me again, as you did in my youth,
Behind the equivocal text the unequivocal truth!

O vintner of Troyes,
Consider the cluster of my time, its form and shape,
And say what wine will issue from this bitter grape!

I wait your answer; in the interim
I do, for you who left no son to read
The prayer before the sacred cherubim,
Intone, as one who is of your male seed,
A Kaddish:
            May it reach eternity
And grace your soul, and even bring some grace
To most unworthy, doubt-divided me.

A Psalm Touching Genealogy

Not sole was I born, but entire genesis:
For to the fathers that begat me, this
Body is residence. Corpuscular,
They dwell in my veins, they eavesdrop at my ear,
They circle, as with Torahs, round my skull,
In exit and in entrance all day pull
The latches of my heart, descend, and rise –
And there look generations through my eyes.

Ballad of the Days of the Messiah

1
O the days of the Messiah are at hand, are at hand!
    The days of the Messiah are at hand!
I can hear the air-raid siren, blow away the age of iron,
    Blast away the age of iron
That was builded on the soft quick-sand.
    O the days of the Messiah are at hand!

2
O Leviathan is ready for the feed, for the feed!
    Leviathan is ready for the feed!
And I hold firm to the credo that both powder and torpedo
    Have so fried that good piscedo
He is ready for the eating, scale and seed!
    Leviathan is ready for the feed!

3
Yea, the sacred wine is ready for the good, for the good,
    The wine of yore intended for the good –

Only all that ruddy water has now turned to blood and slaughter
   Has fermented into slaughter,
Aged for so long, as it has been, in the wood –
   That wine of yore intended for the good!

4

O I see him falling! Will he shoot? Will he shoot?
   Will Messiah's falling herald aim and shoot?
'Tis Elijah, he announces, as he falls from sky, and bounces
   Out of all those silken flounces
Of the heaven-sent and colored parachute:
   Messiah, he is coming, and won't shoot!

5

Don't you hear Messiah coming in his tank, in his tank?
   Messiah in an armor-metalled tank?
I can see the pillared fire, speeding on the metal tire
   Over muck and out of mire
And the seraphim a-shooting from its flank!
   O Messiah, he stands grimy in his tank!

---

from *The Hitleriad*

I

Heil heavenly muse, since also thou must be
Like my song's theme, a sieg-heil'd deity,
Be with me now, but not as once, for song:
Not odes do I indite, indicting Wrong!
Be with me, for I fall from grace to sin,
Spurning this day thy proffered hippocrene,
To taste the poison'd lager of Berlin!

Happier would I be with other themes –
(Who rallies nightmares when he could have dreams?)

With other themes, and subjects more august –
Adolf I sing but only since I must.
I must! Shall I continue the sweet words
That praise the blossoming flowers, the blossoming birds,
While, afar off, I hear the stamping herds?
Shall I, within my ivory tower, sit
And play the solitaire of rhyme and wit,
While Indignation pounds upon the door,
And Pity sobs, until she sobs no more,
And, in the woods, there yelp the hounds of war?

I am the grandson of the prophets! I
Shall not seal lips against iniquity.
Let anger take me in its grasp; let hate,
Hatred of evil prompt me, and dictate!
And let the world see that swastika-stain,
That heart, where no blood is, but high octane,
That little brain –
So that once seen the freak be known again!

Oh, even as his truncheon'd crimes are wrought,
And while the spilt blood is still body-hot,
And even as his doom still seems in doubt,
Let deeds unspeakable be spoken out.
Wherefore, O Muse, I do invoke thy aid,
Not for the light and sweetness of the trade,
But seeing I draw a true bill of the Goth,
For the full fire of thy heavenly wrath!
Aid me, and in good time, for as I talk
The knave goes one step nearer to the dock;
And even as triumphant cannon boom
He marches on his victories – to doom!

II

See him, at last, the culprit twelve men damn.
Is this the face that launched the master-race
And burned the topless towers of Rotterdam?

Why, it's a face like any other face
Among a sea of faces in a mob, –
A peasant's face, an agent's face, no face
At all, no face but vegetarian blob!
The skin's a skin on eggs and turnips fed,
The forehead villainous low, the eyes deepset –
The pervert big eyes of the thwarted bed –
And that mustache, the symbol of the clown
Made emperor, and playing imperial pranks –
Is this the mustache that brought Europe down,
And rolled it flat beneath a thousand tanks?

III

Judge not the man for his face
Out of Neanderthal!
'Tis true 'tis commonplace,
Mediocral,
But the evil of the race
Informs that skull!

You ask, is paragon'd
The Nordic in this thrall?
Why, chivalry's not found
In him at all!
And he's the beast not blond,
Nor is he tall.

His strength is as the strength
Of ten, and ten times ten;
For through him, magnified
Smallness comes to our ken –
The total bigness of
All little men.

XI

Go to *Mein Kampf* if you would know his trade,
And there learn how a people is unmade,
And how, with mocking pantomime,
The tyrants on its ruins climb.
There learn the rules,
(Transparent unto all, save fools)
There take the lessons from the literate boors
And learn to lead the lofty-destined Reich –
Or Barnum-Bailey tours!
Learn it from Adolf's very prosiness,
Indited by his fellow-convict, Hess,
(Though adept at the demagogic yell,
It is averred that Adolf could not spell)
Learn it from him, who, east, west, north and south,
Excelled in the loud bigness of his Mouth!

Learn
How with the double-jointed rhetoric
He turned men's minds – (and stomachs) – and the trick;
Hear him reveal the charlatan's technique:
The prearranged ad-libs, the advisèd shriek,
The spontaneities prepared, the stance
Best suited for prophetic eloquence,
The iterated and ecstatic prose,
And above all, the pose, the Wagnerian pose!
And hear him brief his wisdom, brashly smooth:
'The lie, if oft repeated, is the truth!'

Read, marvelling, the slogans that did foil
The Hun intelligence: Blood, Honour, Soil:
The worship of the blood, in Arians veined,
And in all others preferably uncontained;
The practice of an Honour, modified
By the dear temperature of one's own hide;
And as for Soil, a simple ratio:
Nazis above, all others deep below!

Add then, the insured craft with which he chose
The chosen people for his choicest prose:
Here was a scapegoat to his measure made,
Big enough to inform his wild tirade
And too small to return its foe his due:
The strange ubiquitous Jew!

When could one find a better scapegoat than
The bearded Hebrew cosmopolitan,
Than this the Israelite, not far to seek,
Who was at once an alien, and weak?
Is it the rich who rouse the tribune's ire?
Some Jews are rich, and can well feed his fire.
Is it the poor, the indigent radical?
Judaea's destitution is not small.
The Jew's unsocial – he will not join in
The civic hubbub, the political din,
And also he's too forward; everywhere
Smell his ambitious presence in the air!
Pietist, he pollutes with his old creed
The pagan vigour of the German breed;
And at the same time lifts the mystic mist
From off the German mind – the atheist!
All evil from this Marxian plutocrat:
The Weimar laws, and the Versailles diktat,
The lowered standards and the rising costs,
Inflation and heat-waves, taxes and sharp frosts,
All, all achieved by the Semitic hosts.
The theorem did not matter, nor its flaws, –
Sufficient to sneer 'Jew' to win applause,
Yelp 'Jude,' and await the frenzied jeers –
And thus assure the Reich its thousand years!

So did he still the German hunger with
The ever-novel but right ancient myth,
And taught his people first to heil and hoot,
Then legislate, then doom, then persecute,

Visiting even on the blondest Jew
The crime his great-great-great-grandmother knew!

Such his persuasion, and – the authentic curse –
Such the too-soon persuaded Berliners.
(Observe the method in this madness, since
The Jew being beaten, the world did not wince,
The vogue was shown, by flesh-barometer,
He could persist, yet no great risk incur.)

XV

Yet not by their sole aid did Adolf rise,
His greatest help came from his enemies:
The eye-glass'd Junker looking down
Upon the upstart corporal clown;
The simple Social Democrat;
The Catholic, and concordat;
The too-shrewd plutocratic vons
Thyssen, Hugenberg and sons;
The dialectic theorist who saw the ever-thickening mist
And cheered, in hope that soon therefrom
The light, hegelian, would come;
And even Hindenburg, who in alarm,
Sold a republic for a private farm!

Each in his fashion, and for personal sake
Led Germany to Hitler's stake.
Yes, let it be told, let it be written down
How even from afar
There came the aid that burned the Republic brown;
Let it be told
How gold tycoon, how monied czar,
Reaction black, and Interest, dirty-grey
Trembled before the rumour of that plot
Plotting for Europe its Muscovian day,
And trembling, dropped more coin into the Nazi pot!

Let us not name the names, but let us speak
Only about munition'd dividends,
Of markets rising to an envied peak,
Of rubber's conscienceless elastic ends,
Of timely trains by fascists always mann'd,
And of umbrellas, which, alas, did leak.
Those who have memory will understand.

XXV

But not with human arrogance come I
To plead our Maker's cause, and make His cause
The mighty measure of my feeble words.
Himself, in His good time, the Lord of Hosts,
The slowness of His anger moved at last,
And His longsuffering at last forespent
Will rise, will shine, will stretch forth His right hand
And smite them down, the open impious mouth,
The tongue blaspheming, silenced, in the dust!

I come now rather as a man to men,
Seeking the justice for that voice which cries
Out of the ground, the voice of our brothers' blood!
That blood will not be still again,
Those bones unblessed will still arise,
Yes, and those living spectres, of the mind unhinged,
Will still beat at our padded memory, until
Their fate has been avenged!

XXVI

Let them come forth, those witnesses who stand
Beyond the taunt of perjury, those ghosts
In wagons sealed in a forgotten land,
Murdered; those phantoms the war-tidings boast,
Those skeletons still charred with the gestapo brand!

Let them come forth and speak, who lost their speech
Before the midnight gun-butt on the door,
The men made dumb with their last voiceless screech
In ghetto-yard, and on the Dachau floor, –
Let them accuse now, who did once in vain beseech!

Summon them, bailiff of the dead, the ghosts
Who once were brave men stood against a wall,
Summon them, all the exsanguinated hosts,
Hero and martyr, liquidated; call,
Call forth the witnesses, the uninterrèd ghosts,

And let them speak. And let the dead attest
Their murder and its manner and its cause, –
From shattered jaw, from perforated breast
Speak out their mauling at the bestial claws.
Speak out, or neither we, nor they, again know rest.

Let them in all their thousands speak the shame
Visited on them, and the ignoble death,
The nameless ones, and those of a great fame:
With wounded whisper and with broken breath
Speaking the things unspeakable, and the unspeakable name!

Then from such evidence, such witnessing,
Surely the anger of the world will burst,
Surely the wrath of nations will outfling
Against this culprit, multitude-accursed
Doom indexed by the black gloves of their reckoning!

Thief, perjurer, blasphemer, murderer,
Let him be blotted out, and all his crew.
Efface the evil; let it be no more.
Let the abomination cease; and through
Implacable Justice let emerge the world, clean, new!

Bold malefaction brought at last to bay!
Avenged the martyrs! Mankind truly purged!

Returned at last the spectres to their clay!
And over the green earth, at last emerged,
After the cock-crow of the guns, the cloudless day!

XXVII

And on that day as the unrighteous pass,
Unrighteousness will pass away, and men
Will see once more, as when their vision was
Illumined by the lightning strokes the ten, –
Gesturing Truth ungagged will speak again,
And Man will don his godliness once more –
Then from four corners of the earth will sing
The sons of heaven, the bright freedoms four;
The field will glow again with harvesting,
And glow with argosies the deep; again
Will frolic in the ether, sunlight-blue'd –
Not the grim vulture of the brood
Its talons dripping blood,
But the bright friendly somersaulting plane
Writing against the sky
So all may read on high
Man loyal to his human brotherhood,
To human brotherhood, and to the godly reign!

Autobiographical

1
Out of the ghetto streets where a Jewboy
Dreamed pavement into pleasant bible-land,
Out of the Yiddish slums where childhood met
The friendly beard, the loutish Sabbath-goy,
Or followed, proud, the Torah-escorting band,

Out of the jargoning city I regret,
Rise memories, like sparrows rising from
The gutter-scattered oats,
Like sadness sweet of synagogal hum,
Like Hebrew violins
Sobbing delight upon their eastern notes.

2

Again they ring their little bells, those doors
Deemed by the tender-year'd, magnificent:
Old Ashkenazi's cellar, sharp with spice;
The widows' double-parloured candy-stores
And nuggets sweet bought for one sweaty cent;
The warm fresh-smelling bakery, its pies,
Its cakes, its navel'd bellies of black bread;
The lintels candy-poled
Of barber-shop, bright-bottled, green, blue, red;
And fruit-stall piled, exotic,
And the big synagogue door, with letters of gold.

3

Again my kindergarten home is full –
Saturday night – with kin and compatriot:
My brothers playing Russian card-games; my
Mirroring sisters looking beautiful,
Humming the evening's imminent fox-trot;
My uncle Mayer, of blessed memory,
Still murmuring Maariv, counting holy words;
And the two strangers, come
Fiery from Volhynia's murderous hordes –
The cards and humming stop.
And I too swear revenge for that pogrom.

4

Occasions dear: the four-legged aleph named
And angel pennies dropping on my book;
The rabbi patting a coming scholar-head;
My mother, blessing candles, Sabbath-flamed,

Queenly in her Warsovian perruque;
My father pickabacking me to bed
To tell tall tales about the Baal Shem Tov, –
Letting me curl his beard.
O memory of unsurpassing love,
Love leading a brave child
Through childhood's ogred corridors, unfear'd!

5
The week in the country at my brother's – (May
He own fat cattle in the fields of heaven!)
Its picking of strawberries from grassy ditch,
Its odour of dogrose and of yellowing hay, –
Dusty, adventurous, sunny days, all seven! –
Still follow me, still warm me, still are rich
With the cow-tinkling peace of pastureland.
The meadow'd memory
Is sodded with its clover, and is spanned
By that same pillow'd sky
A boy on his back one day watched enviously.

6
And paved again the street: the shouting boys
Oblivious of mothers on the stoops
Playing the robust robbers and police,
The corn-cob battle, – all high-spirited noise
Competitive among the lot-drawn groups.
Another day, of shaken apple-trees
In the rich suburbs, and a furious dog,
And guilty boys in flight;
Hazelnut games, and games in the synagogue, –
The burrs, the Haman rattle,
The Torah-dance on Simchas-Torah night.

7
Immortal days of the picture-calendar
Dear to me always with the virgin joy
Of the first flowering of senses five,

Discovering birds, or textures, or a star,
Or tastes sweet, sour, acid, those that cloy;
And perfumes. Never was I more alive.
All days thereafter are a dying-off,
A wandering away
From home and the familiar. The years doff
Their innocence.
No other day is ever like that day.

8

I am no old man fatuously intent
On memoirs, but in memory I seek
The strength and vividness of nonage days,
Not tranquil recollection of event.
It is a fabled city that I seek;
It stands in Space's vapours and Time's haze;
Thence comes my sadness in remembered joy
Constrictive of the throat;
Thence do I hear, as heard by a Jewboy
The Hebrew violins,
Delighting in the sobbed oriental note.

Montreal

1

O city metropole, isle riverain!
Your ancient pavages and sainted routs
Traverse my spirit's conjured avenues!
Splendor erablic of your promenades
Foliates there, and there your maisonry
Of pendent balcon and escalier'd march,
Unique midst English habitat,
Is vivid Normandy!

2

You populate the pupils of my eyes:
Thus, does the Indian, plumèd, furtivate
Still through your painted autumns, Ville-Marie!
Though palisades have passed, though calumet
With tabac of your peace enfumes the air,
Still do I spy the phantom, aquiline,
Genuflect, moccasin'd, behind
His statue in the square!

3

Thus, costumed images before me pass,
Haunting your archives architectural:
Coureur de bois, in posts where pelts were portaged;
Seigneur within his candled manoir; Scot
Ambulant through his bank, pillar'd and vast.
Within your chapels, voyaged mariners
Still pray, and personage departed,
All present from your past!

4

Grand port of navigations, multiple
The lexicons uncargo'd at your quays,
Sonnant though strange to me; but chiefest, I,
Auditor of your music, cherish the
Joined double-melodied vocabulaire
Where English vocable and roll Ecossic,
Mollified by the parle of French
Bilinguefact your air!

5

Such your suaver voice, hushed Hochelaga!
But for me also sound your potencies,
Fortissimos of sirens fluvial,
Bruit of manufactory, and thunder
From foundry issuant, all puissant tone
Implenishing your hebdomad; and then

Sanct silence, and your argent belfries
Clamant in orison!

6
You are a part of me, O all your quartiers –
And of dire pauvreté and of richesse –
To finished time my homage loyal claim;
You are locale of infancy, milieu
Vital of institutes that formed my fate;
And you above the city, scintillant,
Mount Royal, are my spirit's mother,
Almative, poitrinate!

7
Never do I sojourn in alien place
But I do languish for your scenes and sounds,
City of reverie, nostalgic isle,
Pendant most brilliant on Laurentian cord!
The coigns of your boulevards – my signiory –
Your suburbs are my exile's verdure fresh,
Yours parks, your fountain'd parks –
Pasture of memory!

8
City, O city, you are vision'd as
A parchemin roll of saecular exploit
Inked with the script of eterne souvenir!
You are in sound, chanson and instrument!
Mental, you rest forever edified
With tower and dome; and in these beating valves,
Here in these beating valves, you will
For all my mortal time reside!

Les Vespasiennes

Dropped privily below the crotch of squares –
its architecture is like the sets in dreams:
the wide slow staircase ... the unknown loiterers ...
the floor that would be counted ... the mirrors' gleams
dancing with daffodils ... and before their white niches
all effigies reversed:
precisely that mise-en-scene, that whiteness which
is seen as having been in dreams seen first:

an anxiety dream where fallen seraphims,
maimed by metabolism, like children of men,
do get their leeching, and rise above their limbs,
and think themselves the angels once again:
and thus, standing in that dream, I and its persons
know at the chemical core,
at the bubbling self, that which was built on and known
even by Vespasian the Emperor,

namely: that we are not God. Not God. Why, not,
not even angels, but something less than men,
creatures, sicknesses, whose pornoglot
identities swim up within our ken
from the *graffiti* behind the amputate door, –
(the wishful drawing and rhyme!)
creatures – the homo, the pervert, the voyeur,
all who grasp love and catch at pantomime.

See how they linger here, while the normal (Who?)
climb up from the subterranean dantesque
into the public square, the shine, the blue,
and don again their feathers and the mask
angelic, and are 'valiant again to cope
with all high enterprise

of true pure love and sweet spiritual hope,'
as if no privies were and only Paradise!

Dentist

The planetary motion of the blood,
Also the peregrinations of routine,
And the bright pendulum of dialectic,
    All go awry,
Lose their direction and their polarhood
    Before the keen
Weltschmerz residing in a cavity!

Sometimes, in such a dire case, this man –
He of the aloe'd pellets against pain –
Has been to my anguish – antiseptic Hero!
    But now, to-day,
I know him different, clumsy Caliban,
    Narcoticized brain,
Gloating with pincers over my dismay!

The panic of his nightmare's still with me:
This ogre of the hypodermic claws,
Smelling of novocaine and drugged mayhem,
    Knee on my chest,
Still runs amok among the ivory,
    Distorts my jaws,
Still keeps my gurgled havoc unexpressed!

May thirty-two curses blight that torturer!
May his gums soften! May he lose his friends
Turning in silence from his exhalations!
    His tinsel wreath

Fall from his mouth, abscessed, with clotted gore
    At its forked ends!
Thirty-two curses on his thirty-two teeth!

Pity he cries? May only thirty-one
Of those foul nibs slip from their gummy curves,
Leaving his food in lumps, uncut, unmolar'd
    For belly's sake –
And may one canine, comic and alone,
    And quick with nerves,
Remain – his weltschmerz and his livelong ache!

Basic English

(To Winston Churchill)

1

Of trope of testament and Caesar's wars
    Grand rhetor, voice
    Of warrior-days,
Not you, I thought, would give the lion's nod
To these eight hundred laboratory mice
Scrawny with fasting, certainly not you
    Of the armada'd phrase!

2

Exporters' argot, small talk of small trade,
    The agent's slang
    Bartering beads,
This is the very speech of nursery blocks,
Pidgin palaver, grunt of Caliban,
By no means the awaited syllables
    For even lesser breeds.

3
Reducing motion to mere come and go,
    Narrowing act
    To give and get,
Flowers no longer flower in the mind;
Fades from the eyes nuance; and eloquence
Sticks in the throat. The dumb are merely raised
    To the inarticulate.

4
Exhausted well of English, and defiled –
    Is it with this
    Semantic spray
You would baptize the cultured continents?
Shall Europe judge and Asia esteem
The wassail liquor of our English speech
    From this, the don's weak tea?

5
In jargoning ports, perhaps, in jungle-river,
    One may make use
    Of such boned gauds:
The drummer, bringing flag and bargain, may
So dragoman himself, perhaps, and thus
Close his shrewd deal, – but only after many
    Gestures, head-shakes, nods.

6
For lettered nations this desesperanto?
    For races that
    Boast alphabet,
And song and synonym and subtlety?
Amused, but polite, the city-dwellers smile;
And that good-will these mumbos were to breed
    We neither – give nor get.

7
For where among the vocables, castrate

Of Saxon strength,
O Sponsor, where
The Hellenic music or the Latin storm?
Where are the thunders of our choric voice?
And where is Shakespeare's scope and Milton's reach?
Your words triphibian, where?

8
Basic as bread, and English as all water –
These bread-and-water
Calories
Are not for men unpainted and in clothes!
O, rather for loincloths on some fronded isle,
Trading at beach, or at the mission chanting –
These skimmed simplicities!

Orator, organist of history, –
Much mightier tones
Have we to sound
Than these flat octaves, playing sad or glad.
Ours is a sweeping measure, resonant,
And destined, for its splendors, not its strictures,
To be renowned!

Bread

Creation's crust and crumb, breaking of bread,
Seedstaff and wheatwand of all miracles,
By your white fiat, at the feast-times said,
World moves, and is revived the shrouded pulse!

Rising, as daily rises the quickening east,
O kneading of knowledge, leaven of happiness,

History yearns upon your yearning yeast!
No house is home without your wifeliness.

No city stands up from its rock-bound knees
Without your rustic aid. None are elect
Save you be common. All philosophies
Betray them with your yokel dialect.

O black-bread hemisphere, oblong of rye,
Crescent and circle of the seeded bun,
All art is builded on your geometry,
All science explosive from your captured sun.

    Bakers most priestly, in your robes of flour,
    White Levites at your altar'd ovens, bind,
    Bind me forever in your ritual, your
    Worship and prayer, me, and all mankind!

And in That Drowning Instant

And in that drowning instant as
the water heightened over me
it suddenly did come to pass
my preterite eternity

the image of myself intent
on several freedoms
               fading to
myself in yellowed Basle-print
vanishing

      into ghetto-Jew
a face among the faces of
the rapt disciples hearkening

the raptures of the Baal Shem Tov
explaining Torah

       vanishing
amidst the water's flickering green

to show me in old Amsterdam
which topples

       into a new scene
Cordova where an Abraham
faces inquisitors

       the face
is suddenly beneath an arch
whose Latin-script the waves erase

and flashes now the backward march
of many

       I among them

       to
Jerusalem-gate and Temple-door!

For the third time my body rises
and finds the good, the lasting shore!

Sonnet Unrhymed

When, on the frustral summit of *extase,*
 – the leaven of my loins to no life spent,
yet vision, as all senses, sharper, – I
peer the vague forward and flawed prism of Time,
many the bodies, my own birthmark bearing,

and many the faces, like my face, I see:
shadows of generation looking backward
and crying *Abba* in the muffled night.

They beg creation. From the far centuries
they move against the vacuum of their murder,
yes, and their eyes are full of such reproach
that although tired, I do wake, and watch
upon the entangled branches of the dark
my sons, my sons, my hanging Absaloms.

Portrait of the Poet as Landscape

I

Not an editorial-writer, bereaved with bartlett,
mourns him, the shelved Lycidas.
No actress squeezes a glycerine tear for him.
The radio broadcast lets his passing pass.
And with the police, no record. Nobody, it appears,
either under his real name or his alias,
missed him enough to report.

It is possible that he is dead, and not discovered.
It is possible that he can be found some place
in a narrow closet, like the corpse in a detective story,
standing, his eyes staring, and ready to fall on his face.
It is also possible that he is alive
and amnesiac, or mad, or in retired disgrace,
or beyond recognition lost in love.

We are sure only that from our real society
he has disappeared; he simply does not count,
except in the pullulation of vital statistics –

somebody's vote, perhaps, an anonymous taunt
of the Gallup poll, a dot in a government table –
but not felt, and certainly far from eminent –
in a shouting mob, somebody's sigh.

O, he who unrolled our culture from his scroll –
the prince's quote, the rostrum-rounding roar –
who under one name made articulate
heaven, and under another the seven-circled air,
is, if he is at all, a number, an x,
a Mr. Smith in a hotel register, –
incognito, lost, lacunal.

II

The truth is he's not dead, but only ignored –
like the mirroring lenses forgotten on a brow
that shine with the guilt of their unnoticed world.
The truth is he lives among neighbours, who, though they will allow
him a passable fellow, think him eccentric, not solid,
a type that one can forgive, and for that matter, forego.

Himself he has his moods, just like a poet.
Sometimes, depressed to nadir, he will think all lost,
will see himself as throwback, relict, freak,
his mother's miscarriage, his great-grandfather's ghost,
and he will curse his quintuplet senses, and their tutors
in whom he put, as he should not have put, his trust.

Then he will remember his travels over that body –
the torso verb, the beautiful face of the noun,
and all those shaped and warm auxiliaries!
A first love it was, the recognition of his own.
Dear limbs adverbial, complexion of adjective,
dimple and dip of conjugation!

And then remember how this made a change in him

affecting for always the glow and growth of his being;
how suddenly was aware of the air, like shaken tinfoil,
of the patents of nature, the shock of belated seeing,
the lonelinesses peering from the eyes of crowds;
the integers of thought; the cube-roots of feeling.

Thus, zoomed to zenith, sometimes he hopes again,
and sees himself as a character, with a rehearsed role:
the Count of Monte Cristo, come for his revenges;
the unsuspected heir, with papers; the risen soul;
or the chloroformed prince awaking from his flowers;
or – deflated again – the convict on parole.

III

He is alone; yet not completely alone.
Pins on a map of a colour similar to his,
each city has one, sometimes more than one:
here, caretakers of art, in colleges;
in offices, there, with arm-bands, and green-shaded;
and there, pounding their catalogued beats in libraries, –

everywhere menial, a shadow's shadow.
And always for their egos – their outmoded art.
Thus, having lost the bevel in the ear,
they know neither up nor down, mistake the part
for the whole, curl themselves in a comma,
talk technics, make a colon their eyes. They distort –

such is the pain of their frustration – truth
to something convolute and cerebral.
How they do fear the slap of the flat of the platitude!
Now Pavlov's victims, their mouths water at bell,
the platter empty.
                        See they set twenty-one jewels
into their watches; the time they do not tell!

Some, patagonian in their own esteem,
and longing for the multiplying word,
join party and wear pins, now have a message,
an ear, and the convention-hall's regard.
Upon the knees of ventriloquists, they own,
of their dandled brightness, only the paint and board.

And some go mystical, and some go mad.
One stares at a mirror all day long, as if
to recognize himself; another courts
angels, – for here he does not fear rebuff;
and a third, alone, and sick with sex, and rapt,
doodles him symbols convex and concave.

O schizoid solitudes! O purities
curdling upon themselves! Who live for themselves,
or for each other, but for nobody else;
desire affection, private and public loves;
are friendly, and then quarrel and surmise
the secret perversions of each other's lives.

IV

He suspects that something has happened, a law
been passed, a nightmare ordered. Set apart,
he finds himself, with special haircut and dress,
as on a reservation. Introvert.
He does not understand this; sad conjecture
muscles and palls thrombotic on his heart.

He thinks an impostor, having studied his personal biography,
his gestures, his moods, now has come forward to pose
in the shivering vacuums his absence leaves.
Wigged with his laurel, that other, and faked with his face,
he pats the heads of his children, pecks his wife,
and is at home, and slippered, in his house.

So he guesses at the impertinent silhouette
that talks to his phone-piece and slits open his mail.
Is it the local tycoon who for a hobby
plays poet, he so epical in steel?
The orator, making a pause? Or is that man
he who blows his flash of brass in the jittering hall?

Or is he cuckolded by the troubadour
rich and successful out of celluloid?
Or by the don who unrhymes atoms? Or
the chemist death built up? Pride, lost impostor'd pride,
it is another, another, whoever he is,
who rides where he should ride.

V

Fame, the adrenalin: to be talked about;
to be a verb; to be introduced as *The*;
to smile with endorsement from slick paper; make
caprices anecdotal; to nod to the world; to see
one's name like a song upon the marquees played;
to be forgotten with embarrassment; to be –
to be.

It has its attractions, but is not the thing;
nor is it the ape mimesis who speaks from the tree
ancestral; nor the merkin joy ...
Rather it is stark infelicity
which stirs him from his sleep, undressed, asleep
to walk upon roofs and window-sills and defy
the gape of gravity.

VI

Therefore he seeds illusions. Look, he is
the nth Adam taking a green inventory

in world but scarcely uttered, naming, praising,
the flowering fiats in the meadow, the
syllabled fur, stars aspirate, the pollen
whose sweet collision sounds eternally.
For to praise

the world – he, solitary man – is breath
to him. Until it has been praised, that part
has not been. Item by exciting item –
air to his lungs, and pressured blood to his heart. –
they are pulsated, and breathed, until they map,
not the world's, but his own body's chart!

And now in imagination he has climbed
another planet, the better to look
with single camera view upon this earth –
its total scope, and each afflated tick,
its talk, its trick, its tracklessness – and this,
this he would like to write down in a book!

To find a new function for the déclassé craft
archaic like the fletcher's; to make a new thing;
to say the word that will become sixth sense;
perhaps by necessity and indirection bring
new forms to life, anonymously, new creeds –
O, somehow pay back the daily larcenies of the lung!

These are not mean ambitions. It is already something
merely to entertain them. Meanwhile, he
makes of his status as zero a rich garland,
a halo of his anonymity,
and lives alone, and in his secret shines
like phosphorus. At the bottom of the sea.

The Rocking Chair

It seconds the crickets of the province. Heard
in the clean lamplit farmhouses of Quebec, –
wooden, – it is no less a national bird;
and rivals, in its cage, the mere stuttering clock.
To its time, the evenings are rolled away;
and in its peace the pensive mother knits
contentment to be worn by her family,
grown-up, but still cradled by the chair in which she sits.

It is also the old man's pet, pair to his pipe,
the two aids of his arithmetic and plans,
plans rocking and puffing into market-shape;
and it is the toddler's game and dangerous dance.
Moved to the verandah, on summer Sundays, it is,
among the hanging plants, the girls, the boy-friends,
sabbatical and clumsy, like the white haloes
dangling above the blue serge suits of the young men.

It has a personality of its own;
is a character (like that old drunk Lacoste,
exhaling amber, and toppling on his pins);
it is alive; individual; and no less
an identity than those about it. And
it is tradition. Centuries have been flicked
from its arcs, alternately flicked and pinned.
It rolls with the gait of St. Malo. It is act

and symbol, symbol of this static folk
which moves in segments, and returns to base, –
a sunken pendulum: *invoke, revoke*;
loosed yon, leashed hither, motion on no space.
O, like some Anjou ballad, all refrain,
which turns about its longing, and seems to move
to make a pleasure out of repeated pain,
its music moves, as if always back to a first love.

The Provinces

First, the two older ones, the bunkhouse brawnymen,
biceps and chest, lumbering over their legend:
scooping a river up in the palm of the hand,
a dangling fish, alive; kicking open a mine;
bashing a forest bald; spitting a country to crop;
for exercise before their boar breakfast,
building a city; racing, to keep in shape,
against the white-sweatered wind; and always
bragging comparisons, and reminiscing
about their fathers' even more mythic prowess,
arguing always, like puffing champions rising
from wrestling on the green.

Then, the three flat-faced blond-haired husky ones.

And the little girl, so beautiful she was named –
to avert the evil of the evil eye –
after a prince, not princess. In crossed arms cradling her,
her brothers, tanned and long-limbed.
(Great fishermen, hauling out of Atlantic
their catch and their coal
and netting with appleblossom the shoals of their sky.)

And, last, as if of another birth,
the hunchback with the poet's face; and eyes
blue as the glass he looks upon; and fruit
his fragrant knuckles and joints; of iron marrow; –
affecting always a green habit, touched with white.

Nine of them; not counting
the adopted boy of the golden complex, nor
the proud collateral albino, – nine,
a sorcery of numbers, a game's stances.

But the heart seeks one, the heart, and also the mind
seeks single the thing that makes them one, if one.
        Yet where shall one find it? In their history –
the cairn of cannonball on the public square?
Their talk, their jealous double-talk? Or in
the whim and weather of a geography
curling in drifts about the forty-ninth?
Or find it in the repute of character:
romantic as mounties? Or discover it
in beliefs that say:
this is a country of Christmas trees?
           Or hear it sing
from the house with towers, from whose towers ring
bells, and the carillon of laws?
Where shall one find it? What
to name it, that is sought?
The ladder the nine brothers hold by rungs?
The birds that shine on each other? The white water
that foams from the ivy entering their eaves?

Or find it, find it, find it commonplace
but effective, valid, real, the unity
in the family feature, the not unsimilar face?

The Cripples

(Oratoire de St. Joseph)

Bundled their bones, upon the ninetynine stairs –
St. Joseph's ladder – the knobs of penance come;
the folded cripples counting up their prayers.

How rich, how plumped with blessing is that dome!
The gourd of Brother André! His sweet days
rounded! Fulfilled! Honeyed to honeycomb!

Whither the heads, upon the ninetynine trays,
the palsied, who double their aspen selves, the lame,
the unsymmetrical, the dead-limbed, raise

their look, their hope, and the *idée fixe* of their maim, –
knowing the surgery's in the heart. Are not
the ransomed crutches worshippers? And the fame

of the brother sanatorial to this plot? –
God mindful of the sparrows on the stairs?
Yes, to their faith this mountain of stairs, is not!

They know, they know, that suddenly their cares
and orthopedics will fall from them, and they
stand whole again.

       Roll empty away, wheelchairs,
and crutches, without armpits, hop away!

And I who in my own faith once had faith like this,
but have not now, am crippled more than they.

The Snowshoers

The jolly icicles ringing in their throats,
their mouths meerschaums of vapour,
from the saints' parishes they come, like snowmen
spangled, with spectrum colour
patching the scarf green, sash red, sky-blue the coat –
come to the crystal course. Their airy hooves
unslung from their backs are ready
to stamp their goodlucks on the solid foam.
Till then, the saints all heralded,
they snowball their banter below the angular eaves.

O gala garb, bright with assomption, flags
on limb and torso curled –
furling of white, blue zigzags, rondures red!
A candy-coloured world!
And moods as primary as their tuques and togs, –
of tingling cold, and the air rubbed down with snow
and winter well-being!
Like a slapdash backdrop, the street moves with colours,
the zones and rhomboids moving
toward the enhancing whiteness of the snow.

And now, clomping the packed-down snow of the street
they walk on sinews
gingerly, as if their feet were really swollen,
eager for release
from the blinders of buildings; suddenly they cut
a corner, and – the water they will walk!
Surf of the sun!
World of white wealth! Wind's tilth! Waves
of dazzling dominion
on which their coloured sails will billow and rock!

For the Sisters of the Hotel Dieu

In pairs,
as if to illustrate their sisterhood,
the sisters pace the hospital garden walks.
In their robes black and white immaculate hoods
they are like birds,
the safe domestic fowl of the House of God.

O biblic birds,
who fluttered to me in my childhood illnesses

– me little, afraid, ill, not of your race, –
the cool wing for my fever, the hovering solace,
the sense of angels –
be thanked, O plumage of paradise, be praised.

Grain Elevator

Up from the low-roofed dockyard warehouses
it rises blind and babylonian
like something out of legend. Something seen
in a children's coloured book. Leviathan
swamped on our shore? The cliffs of some other river?
The blind ark lost and petrified? A cave
built to look innocent, by pirates? Or
some eastern tomb a travelled patron here makes local?

But even when known, it's more than what it is:
for here, as in a Josephdream, bow down
the sheaves, the grains, the scruples of the sun
garnered for darkness; and Saskatchewan
is rolled like a rug of a thick and golden thread.
O prison of prairies, ship in whose galleys roll
sunshines like so many shaven heads,
waiting the bushel-burst out of the beached bastille!

Sometimes, it makes me think Arabian,
the grain picked up, like tic-tacs out of time:
first one; an other; singly; one by one; –
to save life. Sometimes, some other races claim
the twinship of my thought, – as the river stirs
restless in a white Caucasian sleep,
or, as in the steerage of the elevators,
the grains, Mongolian and crowded, dream.

A box: cement, hugeness, and rightangles –
merely the sight of it leaning in my eyes
mixes up continents and makes a montage
of inconsequent time and uncontiguous space.
It's because it's bread. It's because
bread is its theme, an absolute. Because
always this great box flowers over us
with all the coloured faces of mankind ...

Université de Montréal

Faculté de Droit

Flaunting their canes, their jaunty berets, the students throng
slick serpentine the street and streamer the air
with ribbons of ribaldry and bunting song.
Their faces, shadowed seminary-pale,
open, flash red, announce their epaulettes,
escape from Xenophon and old Virgile.
Gaily they wind and stagger towards their own
and through the maze already see themselves
silken and serious, a gownèd guild
a portrait painter will one day make traditional
beneath the Sign of the *Code Napoléon*.

This, then, their last permitted juvenal mood
kicked up by adolescence before it dons
the crown and dignity of adulthood.
Today, the grinning circle on the *Place d'Armes*,
mock trial, thumbdown'd verdict, and, singsong,
the joyous sentence of death; tomorrow, the
good of the state, the law, the dean
parting deliberate his beard
silvered and sabled with rampant right and wrong.

Thus will they note in notebooks, and will con
the numbers and their truths, and from green raw
celebrants of the Latin Quarter, duly
warp and wrinkle into *avocats.*
The solid men. Now innocence and fun.
O let them have their day, it soon will go!
Soon are begun
for haggler and schemer and electioneer –
the wizened one who is a library key,
the fat one plumped upon the *status quo* –
the fees and fetters of career.
Soon they enter
their twenty diaries, clocked and elaborate,
and soon, too soon, begin to live to leave
en bon père de famille, – a sound estate.

The Sugaring

For Guy Sylvestre

Starved, scarred, lenten, amidst ash of air,
roped and rough-shirted, the maples in the unsheltered grove
after their fasts and freezings stir.
Ah, winter for each one,
each gospel tree, each saint of the calendar,
has been a penance, a purchase: the nails of ice!
wind's scourge! the rooted cross!
Nor are they done with the still stances of love,
the fiery subzeros of sacrifice.

For standing amidst the thorns of their own bones,
eased by the tombs' coolth of resurrection time, –
the pardon, the purgatorial groans

almost at bitter end,
but not at end – the carving auger runs
spiral the round stigmata through each limb!
The saints bleed down their sides!
And look! men catch this juice of their agonized prime
to boil in kettles the sap of seraphim!

O, out of this calvary Canadian comes bliss,
savour and saving images of holy things,
a sugared metamorphosis!
Ichor of dulcitude
shaping sweet relics, crystalled spotlessness!
And the pious pour into the honeyed dies
the sacred hearts, the crowns,
thanking those saints for syrops of their dying
and blessing the sweetness of their sacrifice.

Indian Reservation: Caughnawaga

Where are the braves, the faces like autumn fruit,
who stared at the child from the coloured frontispiece?
And the monosyllabic chief who spoke with his throat?
Where are the tribes, the feathered bestiaries? –
Rank Aesop's animals erect and red,
with fur on their names to make all live things kin! –
Chief Running Deer, Black Bear, Old Buffalo Head?

Childhood, that wished me Indian, hoped that
one afterschool I'd leave the classroom chalk,
the varnish smell, the watered dust of the street,
to join the clean outdoors and the Iroquois track.
Childhood; but always, – as on a calendar, –
there stood that chief, with arms akimbo, waiting
the runaway mascot paddling to his shore.

With what strange moccasin stealth that scene is changed!
With French names, without paint, in overalls,
their bronze, like their nobility expunged, –
the men. Beneath their alimentary shawls
sit like black tents their squaws; while for the tourist's
brown pennies scattered at the old church door,
the ragged papooses jump, and bite the dust.

Their past is sold in a shop: the beaded shoes,
the sweetgrass basket, the curio Indian,
burnt wood and gaudy cloth and inch-canoes –
trophies and scalpings for a traveller's den.
Sometimes, it's true, they dance, but for a bribe;
after a deal don the bedraggled feather
and welcome a white mayor to the tribe.

This is a grassy ghetto, and no home.
And these are fauna in a museum kept.
The better hunters have prevailed. The game,
losing its blood, now makes these grounds its crypt.
The animals pale, the shine of the fur is lost,
bleached are their living bones. About them watch
as through a mist, the pious prosperous ghosts.

Krieghoff: Calligrammes

Let the blank whiteness of this page be snow
and majuscule the make of Cornelius:
    then tented A's inverted V's
may circumflex and shade the paysage page
    with French-Canadian trees;
or equal the arrows of the frozen flow
    by the last minus of degrees

stopped in their flight; or show
the wigwams and the gables –
of Krieghoff the pat petted verities.

And any signs will do:
the ladder H that prongs above the chimney;
prone J's on which the gay sleighs run;
the Q and her papoose;
crucifix Y; or bosomed farmwife B –
wanting an easel and the painter's flourish
with alphabet make free,
make squares, make curlecues
of his simplicity.

But colours? Ah, the two colours!

These must be spun, these must be bled
out of the iris of the intent sight:
red rufous roseate crimson russet red
     blank   candid   white.

Political Meeting

(For Camillien Houde)

On the school platform, draping the folding seats,
they wait the chairman's praise and glass of water.
Upon the wall the agonized Y initials their faith.

Here all are laic; the skirted brothers have gone.
Still, their equivocal absence is felt, like a breeze
that gives curtains the sounds of surplices.

The hall is yellow with light, and jocular;
suddenly some one lets loose upon the air
the ritual bird which the crowd in snares of singing

catches and plucks, throat, wings, and little limbs.
Fall the feathers of sound, like *alouette's*.
The chairman, now, is charming, full of asides and wit,

building his orators, and chipping off
the heckling gargoyles popping in the hall.
(Outside, in the dark, the street is body-tall,

flowered with faces intent on the scarecrow thing
that shouts to thousands the echoing
of their own wishes.) The Orator has risen!

Worshipped and loved, their favourite visitor,
a country uncle with sunflower seeds in his pockets,
full of wonderful moods, tricks, imitative talk,

he is their idol: like themselves, not handsome,
not snobbish, not of the *Grande Allée! Un homme!*
Intimate, informal, he makes bear's compliments

to the ladies; is gallant; and grins;
goes for the balloon, his opposition, with pins;
jokes also on himself, speaks of himself

in the third person, slings slang, and winks with folklore;
and knows now that he has them, kith and kin.
Calmly, therefore, he begins to speak of war,

praises the virtue of being *Canadien*,
of being at peace, of faith, of family,
and suddenly his other voice: *Where are your sons?*

He is tearful, choking tears; but not he
would blame the clever English; in their place
he'd do the same; maybe.

Where *are* your sons?
                    The whole street wears one face,
shadowed and grim; and in the darkness rises
the body-odour of race.

Frigidaire

Even in July it is our winter corner,
hill 70 of our kitchen, rising white
and cool to the eye, cool to the alpenfinger.
The shadows and wind of snowfall fall from its sides.

And when the door swings away, like a cloud blown,
the village is Laurentian, tiered and bright,
with thresholds of red, white roofs, and scattered greens;
and it has a sky, and clouds, and a northern light.

Is peopled. On its vallied streets there stands
a bevy of milk, coifed like the sisters of snow;
and beaded bosoms of butter; and red farmhands;
all poised, as if to hear from the distant meadow,

there on the heights, with its little flowers of white,
the cubes that seem to sound like pasture bells.
Fixed to that far-off tingle they don't quite
hear, they stand, frozen with eavesdropping, like icicles.

And there on the heights, the storm's electric, thriving
with muffled thunder, and lightning slow and white!
It is a private sky, a weather exclusive,
a slow, sensational, and secret sight.

Dress Manufacturer: Fisherman

In his wandered wharf on the brake side of the lake;
in boots bucolic;
thatched and eaved with brim and circle of straw,
he'll sit for hours, himself his boat's prow
dangling the thread of his preoccupation.

Far from the lint and swatches, among lilies
chinned upon glass,
among the bulrushes his childhood only read, –
over cool corridors
pearled with bubbles, speckled with trout,
beneath the little songs, the little wings,
his city ardours all go out
into the stipple and smooth of natural things.

And he becomes, at the end of his filament,
a correspondent of water and of fish,
one who casts line and riches –
the glittering foolish spoon the rainbow fly –
to hide within the wish
that for so many years beat from the heat
of his enterprise and city sky
the simmering emphasis of his summer loss.

Here he would sink the curbstones!
And on the granite of his effort
grow a moss!

Back to the hotel, tanned, percer-proud
with the ransom of his youth –

a hero with private trout –
he's familiar in the kitchen, a fisherman
all evening in the lobby kidded and praised;
is modest, but encourages talk; and knows
with every compliment and trout
his childhood summers from the water raised.

The Break-up

They suck and whisper it in mercury,
the thermometers. It is shouted red
from all the Aprils hanging on the walls.
In the dockyard stalls
the stevedores, their hooks rusty, wonder; the
wintering sailors in the taverns bet.

A week, and it will crack! Here's money that
a fortnight sees the floes, the smokestacks red!
Outside *The Anchor's* glass, St. Lawrence lies
rigid and white and wise,
nor ripple and dip, but fathom-frozen flat.
There are no hammers will break that granite lid.

But it will come! Some dead of night with boom
to wake the wagering city, it will break,
will crack, will melt its muscle-bound tides
and raise from their iced tomb
the pyramided fish, the unlockered ships,
and last year's blue and bloated suicides.

Winter Night: Mount Royal

Slowly, and flake by flake ... At the drifted frond
of the terraces and ski-runs over me
there falls a snow of sound:
tinkle of frost   minims of mercury
        campanile cold

Horseman and horse among the chandeliers
parting the crystal twigs? Some belfry burst
frozen, and fractured into chips of sound?
The air itself
made little globes,
their rounds ringing in Fahrenheit descant?

White innocence the mountainside is mist,
its bells as secret as the bells of its flowers.

Now nearer, and jollier, and fourtimed, canters
the bend of the road this jingle of this silver!
Big-eyed, equestrian, trotting
the nickle blossoms,
the bells and hellos of his yoke and harness!

Heraldic, guled, the sleigh in a flurry of sound –
hooves upon snow the falsettos of water
and bells cavalier –
passes before me, is festive, and passes beyond
the curve of the road, the heels of its runners
scrolling it into the mist.

They are now fainter, have no direction, lost.
One would say the hidden stars were bells
dangling between the shafts of the Zodiac.
One would say
the snowflakes falling clinked together their sparkles

to make these soft, these satin-muffled
tintinnabulations.

Lookout: Mount Royal

Remembering boyhood, it is always here
the boy in blouse and kneepants on the road
trailing his stick over the hopscotched sun;
or here, upon the suddenly moving hill;
or at the turned tap its cold white mandarin mustaches;
or at the lookout, finally,
breathing easy, standing still

to click the eye on motion forever stopped:
the photographer's tripod and his sudden faces
buoyed up by water on his magnet caught
still smiling as if under water still;
the exclamatory tourists descending the caleches;
the maids in starch; the ladies in white gloves;
other kids of other slums and races;
and on the bridle-paths
the horsemen on their horses like the tops of f's:

or from the parapet make out
beneath the green marine
the discovered road, the hospital's romantic
gables and roofs, and all the civic Euclid
running through sunken parallels and lolling
in diamond and square, then proud-pedantical
with spire and dome
making its way to the sought point, his home.

home recognized: there: to be returned to –

lets the full birdseye circle to the river,
its singsong bridges, its mapmaker curves, its
island with the two shades of green, meadow and wood;
and circles round that water-tower'd coast;
then, to the remote rhapsodic mountains; then,
 – and to be lost –
to clouds like white slow friendly animals
which all the afternoon across his eyes
will move their paced spaced footfalls.

The Mountain

Who knows it only by the famous cross which bleeds
into the fifty miles of night its light
knows a night-scene;
and who upon a postcard knows its shape –
the buffalo straggled of the laurentian herd, –
holds in his hand a postcard.

In layers of mountains the history of mankind,
and in Mount Royal
which daily in a streetcar I surround
my youth, my childhood –
the pissabed dandelion, the coolie acorn,
green prickly husk of chestnut beneath mat of grass –
O all the amber afternoons
are still to be found.

There is a meadow, near the pebbly brook,
where buttercups, like once on the under of my chin
upon my heart still throw their rounds of yellow.

And Cartier's monument, based with nude figures
still stands where playing hookey

Lefty and I tested our gravel aim
(with occupation flinging away our guilt)
against the bronze tits of Justice.

And all my Aprils there are marked and spotted
upon the adder's tongue, darting in light,
upon the easy threes of trilliums, dark green, green, and white,
threaded with earth, and rooted
beside the bloodroots near the leaning fence –
corms and corollas of childhood,
a teacher's presents.

And chokecherry summer clowning black on my teeth!

The birchtree stripped by the golden zigzag still
stands at the mouth of the dry cave where I
one suppertime in August watched the sky
grow dark, the wood quiet, and then suddenly spill
from barrels of thunder and broken staves of lightning –
terror and holiday!

One of these days I shall go up to the second terrace
to see if it still is there –
the uncomfortable sentimental bench
where, – as we listened to the brass of the band concerts
made soft and to our mood by dark and distance –
I told the girl I loved
I loved her.

Lone Bather

Upon the ecstatic diving board the diver,
poised for parabolas, lets go
lets go his manshape to become a bird.

Is bird, and topsy-turvy
the pool floats overhead, and the white tiles snow
their crazy hexagons. Is dolphin. Then
is plant with lilies bursting from his heels.

Himself, suddenly mysterious and marine,
bobs up a merman leaning on his hills.

Plashes and plays alone the deserted pool;
as those, is free, who think themselves unseen.
He rolls in his heap of fruit,
he slides his belly over
the melonrinds of water, curved and smooth and green.
Feels good: and trains, like little acrobats
his echoes dropping from the galleries;
circles himself over a rung of water;
swims fancy and gay; taking a notion, hides
under the satins of his great big bed, –
and then comes up to float until he thinks
the ceiling at his brow, and nowhere any sides.

His thighs are a shoal of fishes: scattered: he
turns with many gloves of greeting
towards the sunnier water and the tiles.

Upon the tiles he dangles from his toes
lazily the eight reins of his ponies.

An afternoon, far from the world
a street sound throws like a stone, with paper, through the glass.
Up, he is chipped enamel, grained with hair.
The gloss of his footsteps follows him to the showers,
the showers, and the male room, and the towel
which rubs the bird, the plant, the dolphin back again
personable plain.

Pastoral of the City Streets

I

Between distorted forests, clapped into geometry,
in meadows of macadam,
heat-fluff-a-host-of-dandelions dances on the air.
Everywhere glares the sun's glare,
the asphalt shows hooves.
                              In meadows of macadam
grazes the dray horse, nozzles his bag of pasture,
is peaceful. Now and then flicks through farmer straw
his ears, like pulpit-flowers; quivers
his hide; swishes his tempest tail
a black and sudden nightmare for the fly.
The sun shines, sun shines down
new harness on his withers, saddle, and rump.

On curbrock and on stairstump the clustered kids
resting let slide some afternoon: then restless
hop to the game of the sprung haunches; skid
to the safe place; jump up: stir a wind in the heats:
laugh, puffed and sweat-streaked.

O for the crystal stream!

Comes a friend's father
with his pet of a hose,
and plays the sidewalk black
cavelike and cool.

O crisscross beneath the spray, those pelting petals and peas
those white soft whisks
brushing off heat!
O underneath these acrobatic fountains
among the crystal,

like raindrops a sunshower of youngsters dance:
small-nippled self-hugged boys
and girls with water sheer, going *Ah* and *Ah*.

II

And at twilight,
the sun like a strayed neighbourhood creature
having been chased
back to its cover
the children count a last game, or talk, or rest,
beneath the bole of the tree of the single fruit of glass
now ripening,
a last game, talk, or rest,
until mothers like evening birds call from the stoops.

M. Bertrand

Oh, but in France they arrange these things much better!
M. Bertrand who always, before kissing the female wrist
rolls the *r* in *charmante*
admits he owes everything to those golden Sorbonne years.
Returned now to our forest, he is sad and nostalgic;
indeed, pained; he winces when his brother says *icitte*.
O, he can never forget fair Paris, its culture and cuisine,
particularly as he stalks deaf and hungry
among the barbarians who never were seasick.
     Still, he has one consolation – the visitor from abroad,
the old classmate, the *conférencier*, perhaps, even
a bearded *maître* of the Academy.
Then is he revived, like a dotard by the *Folies Bergères*,
revived, stimulated, made loquacious with *argot*,

and can't do enough for his guest, but would lavish on him
jowl-kiss, hand-kiss, and other kisses Parisian.

Monsieur Gaston

You remember the big Gaston, for whom everyone predicted
a bad end? –
Gaston, the neighbour's gossip and his mother's cross?
You remember him *vaurien*, always out of a job,
with just enough clinking coinage
for pool, bright neckties, and blondes, –
the scented Gaston in the poolroom lolling
in meadows of green baize?
In clover now. Through politics. *Monsieur* Gaston.

They say the Minister of a certain department does not move
without him; and they say, to make it innocent, –
chauffeur.
But everyone understands. Why, wherever our Gaston smiles
a nightclub rises and the neons flash.
To his slightest whisper
the bottled rye, like a fawning pet-dog, gurgles.
The burlesque queen will not undress
unless Monsieur Gaston says yes.
And the Madame will shake her head behind the curtain-rods
unless he nods.

A changed man, Gaston; almost a civil servant,
keeps records, appointments, women; speaks tough English;
is very much respected.
You should hear with what greetings his distinguished approach
   is greeted;
you should see the gifts he gets,
with compliments for his season.

Doctor Drummond

It is to be wondered whether he ever really
saw them, whether he knew them more than type,
whether, in fact, his occupational fun –
the doctor hearty over his opened grip –
did not confuse him into deducing
his patients' health and Irish from his own.

Certainly from his gay case-histories
that now
for two-tongued get-togethers are elocutional,
one would never have recognized his clientele.

Consider this patrician patronizing the *patois,*
consider his *habitants,* the homespun of their minds and motives,
and you will see them as he saw them – as *white* natives,
characters out of comical Quebec,
of speech neither Briton nor Breton, a fable folk,
a second class of aborigines,
docile, domesticate, very good employees,
so meek that even their sadness
made dialect for a joke.

One can well imagine the doctor,
in club, in parlour, or in smoking car,
building out of his practise a reputation
as raconteur.
But the true pulsing of their blood
his beat ignores,
and of the temperature of their days, the chills
of their despairs, the fevers of their faith,
his mercury is silent.

Parade of St. Jean Baptiste

Bannered, and ranked, and at its stances fixed
the enfilade with vestment colours the air.
Roll now the batons of the tambours round
ruminant with commencement, and now sound
annunciative, ultramontane, the
fanfares of jubilee!
It moves: festive and puissant the chivalry
advances chief, law crouped and curvetting –
finish and force, undulant muscle and braid –
O centaurs en gambade!

They move as through a garden, moving between
gay altitudes of flowers, populous
of all the wards and counties burgeoning here:
ribbons and countenances, joys and colours –
nuances of meridian, the blue,
the rose, the vert, the blond, all lambencies
to this rich spectacle turned heliotropic,
graceful and levitant: Quebec, its people:
flotation of faces; badinage of petals:
profound from suburbs surfaced on
the Real to spy Imagination.

Applause! Ovation of hourras! There pass
before the flowering faces, imaged, the
animal fables, myths of the crayon'd class,
the nursery's voyage and discovery:
redeemed and painted is the Indian;
lake sirens chant again; and sorcery
again makes princess out of Cendrillon,
(by Massicotte, research; and courtesy
of Simpson's and of Eaton T. and Son)
last! last! the coachmen of *chasse-galerie*.

Oh, all, – parents, their infant epaulettes –
Here all are dauphins of a vanished empery.

The grand progenitor! Hébert! Salute
as acted en tableau revivified
the pioneer fiat, the patrimonial geste
deracinating forest into prairie!
Surge, visions of farms the river parcelled out!
Conjured, the parish parallelograms,
the chapel's verdant foyer! (Does not this scene,
habitants of the fumed and pulverous city
immured in granite canyons and constrict,
does it not veil the eyes with memories
sylvan, campestral? Does it not palpitate pain
current nostalgic away from the factory
to the mountain liberties and large champaign?)

Now, into their vision, from the parishes
with gonfalons emergent juvenal
the schools and seminaries, potent with race:
name after name, catena of grand fame,
tradition-orgulous. Martyr and saint
chrysostomate their standards. Aspiration
surrounds them, and the future dowers with power –
regenerate, augmentative: the nation.
The berceuses are its anthems; thus survives
philoprogenitive Quebec; thus grants survival
unto the spired culture elsewhere tomb'd.
Yes, here with students and their cassock'd doctors,
the angels of Aquinas dance their dances,
and march the pious mascots of St. Francis.

Quebec, Quebec, which for the long blanched age –
infidelium partes – multiplied
pagan its beasts and painted savages –
(while Rome was rounded with St. Peter's dome
and Europe vertical with tower and cross
supported constellations) – is still rich

of realms spiritual the Jesuits founded,
and Sabbaths of the monks of Yamachiche.
Crosses of clergy, luxe armorial,
still vivify with their insignia
the evangelical air, and benedictions
douce-digital from priest and eminence
still quadrilate the inhospitable tense.

And sudden! camaraderie and jokes.
Ablute and pompous, staid, the rotund mayor
(remember in Maisonneuve his gestured discourse –
Cyrano, né p'tit gars de Ste. Marie?)
with chain of office now, and magistral,
promenades, flanked by seniors of the city.
These are not allegorical; the people
familiar, still, as if with candidates,
cry out allusions, scandals; parodize
the clichés and the rhetoric suave.
But unconcerned and bland, the marked elect
march recognitions through the colonnade –
ineffably correct.

Patronial, of recent heraldry:
the piston sinistral, the scutcheon coin,
blazon and bar of bank, – the seigneurie
of capital, new masters of domain.
See, this is he, the pulp magnifico,
and this the nabob of the northern mine;
this man is pelts, and this man men allow
factotum. To the servants of their wage,
le peup', the docile, the incognito
paupers, they do offer the day's homage,
but know their seasons appertain to them,
they being loyal, inexpensive, liege.

O who can measure the potency of symbols?
The hieratic gesture murdering grief?
The gloss on suffering? The jewelled toy

that sports away quotidian the anguish?
For the grey seasons and the frustrate heart,
therefore, these rituals, which are therapy,
a ceremonial appeasement. O
single and sole upon the calendar
the baptist's day with rite and rapture tints
dolor that for its annuair of days
will dance, refract, this one day's images.

Departed is the enfilade; the people
in groups chromatic through the boulevards
disperse; spectators benched and poled, descend;
the traffic gauntlets gesture; klaxons sound;
all motion is pastelled; gala and gay
the picnic-loud tramway.
It is a prelude for the pleiades
that pyrotechnic will this night illume
pères de famille idyllic and content,
and in the dense boskage the ancient intimate experiment.

Cantabile

De litteris, et de armis, praestantibusque ingeniis

And when they brought him back
the fibbiest fabricator of them all
     il miglior fabbro
they didn't know what to do with him
     at the customs he had had nothing to declare
saving and except a number of synonyms, to wit:
zhid, sheeny, jewboy, youpin, kike, yitt, shweef.
             and the ballad
   But bye and rade the Black Douglas
   And wow but he was rough!

> For he pulled up the bonny brier
> And flang't in St. Mary's Lough.

didn't know what to do with him ... hang him?
old, *exhaussé*, a poet, there was a question of ethics, moreover
         one kuddent make a martyr of him, cood one?
               St. Ezra Benedict

So the seven psychiatrists feigned insanity
committed him.

U S U R A: that his offence
that he sought to extract an exorbitant interest
                     from a limited talent.
speculated in the culture exchanges
passed off   χρύσω   χρυσοτέρα
the Dante coinage, Provençal, Chinese yen
not as his own, but his for increment.

It must be admitted, however, that as a pawnbroker
he was distinguished.
He invented a new way to ring a coin on the table
was expert in the bite for counterfeit,
trafficked only in the best mdse. and to his friends gave discounts
for the rest was fierce, bearded like the pard, like his Jew.
         Pound   Libra   £

USURA

The cantos? 'The art of conversation' said Tate (Allen) meaning
small talk shouted.
80 of them 80
anecdote, persiflage, ideogram, traduction
             traductore – tradittore
all to the same if any effect – the syphilisation of our gonorera
            and Pound its thunder clap,
a good role but the wrong actor.

Don't you think said the lady from Idaho on tour at Rapallo
that he will be remembered?   Yes
As the author of a Gradus ad parnassum
    "   a compiler of several don'ts
    "   a perpetrator of ditto
    "   a dropper-down of learning's crumbs
 and as the stoic of the empty portals.

Otherwise, as Jimmy, quoting himself and poor Mr. Breen
           E.P.: EP
           'EP.   *Est Perditus.*

Sestina on the Dialectic

Yes yeasts to No, and No is numinous with Yes. All is a hap, a
haze, a hazard, a do-doubtful, a flight from, a travel to. Nothing
will keep, but eases essence, – out! – outplots its plight. So westers
east, and so each teaches an opposite: a nonce-thing still.

A law? Fact or flaw of the fiat, still – a law. It binds us,
braided, wicker and withe. It stirs the seasons, it treads the tides, it
so rests in our life there's nothing, there's not a sole thing that
from its workings will not out.

The antics of the antonyms! From, to; stress, slack, and
stress, – a rhythm running to a reason, a double dance, a shivering
still.

Even the heart's blood, bursting in, bales out, an ebb and flow;
and even the circuit within which its pulsebeat's beam –man's
morse – is a something that grows, that grounds, – treks, totters. So.

O dynasties and dominions downfall so! Flourish to flag and
fail, are potent to a pause, a panic precipice, to a picked pit, and

thence – rubble rebuilding, – still rise resurrective, – and now see them, with new doers in dominion!

They, too, dim out.

World's sudden with somersault, updown, inout, overandunder. And, note well: also that other world, the two-chambered mind, goes with it, ever kaleidoscopic, one scape to another, suffering change that changes still, that focusses and fissions *the* to *a*.

When will there be arrest? Consensus? A marriage of the antipathies, and out of the vibrant deaths and rattles the life still? O just as the racked one hopes his ransom, so I hope it, name it, image it, the together-living, the together-with, the final synthesis. A stop.

But so it never will turn out, returning to the rack within, without. And no thing's still.

Meditation upon Survival

At times, sensing that the golgotha'd dead
run plasma through my veins, and that I must live
their unexpired six million circuits, giving
to each of their nightmares my body for a bed –
inspirited, dispirited –
those times that I feel their death-wish bubbling the
channels of my blood –
I grow bitter at my false felicity –
the spared one – and would almost add my wish
for the centigrade furnace and the cyanide flood.

However, one continues to live, though mortally.
O, like some frightened, tattered, hysterical man

run to a place of safety – the whole way run –
whose lips, now frenzy-foamed, now delirium-dry,
cry out the tenses of the verb to die,
cry love, cry loss, being asked: *And yet unspilled
your own blood?* weeps, and makes
his stuttering innocence a kind of guilt –
O, like that man am I, bereaved and suspect,
convicted with the news my mourning breaks.

Us they have made the monster, made that thing
that lives though cut in three: the severed head
which breathes, looks on, hears, thinks, weeps, and is bled
continuously with a drop by drop longing
for its members' re-membering!
And, the torn torso, spilling heart and lights
and the cathartic dregs!
These, for the pit! Upon the roads, the flights –
– O how are you reduced, my people, cut down to a limb! –
upon the roads the flights of the bodiless legs.

Myself to recognize: a curio;
the atavism of some old coin's face;
one who, though watched and isolate, does go –
the last point of a diminished race –
the way of the fletched buffalo.
Gerundive of extinct. An original.
What else, therefore, to do
but leave these bones that are not ash to fill –
O not my father's vault – but the glass-case
some proud museum catalogues *Last Jew.*

Elegy

Named for my father's father, cousin, whose cry
Might have been my cry lost in that dark land –

Where shall I seek you? On what wind shall I
Reach out to touch the ash that was your hand?
The Atlantic gale and the turning of the sky
Unto the cubits of my ambience
Scatter the martyr-motes. Flotsam-of-flame!
God's image made the iotas of God's name!
O through a powder of ghosts I walk; through dust
Seraphical upon the dark winds borne;
Daily I pass among the sieved white hosts,
Through clouds of cousinry transgress,
Maculate with the ashes that I mourn.
   Where shall I seek you? There's not anywhere
A tomb, a mound, a sod, a broken stick,
Marking the sepulchres of those sainted ones
The dogfaced hid in tumuli of air.
O cousin, cousin, you are everywhere!
And in your death, in your ubiquity,
Bespeak them all, our sundered cindered kin:
David, whose cinctured bone –
Young branch once wreathed in phylactery! –
Now hafts the peasant's bladed kitchenware;
And the dark Miriam murdered for her hair;
And the dark Miriam murdered for her hair;
The relicts nameless; and the tattoo'd skin
Fevering from lampshade in a cultured home, –
All, all our gaunt skull-shaven family –
The faces are my face! that lie in lime,
You bring them, jot of horror, here to me,
Them, and the slow eternity of despair
That tore them, and did tear them out of time.

Death may be beautiful, when full of years,
Ripe with good works, a man, among his sons,
Says his last word, and turns him to the wall.
But not these deaths! O not these weighted tears!
The flesh of thy sages, Lord, flung prodigal
To the robed fauna with their tubes and shears;
Thy chosen for a gold tooth chosen; for
The pervert's wetness, flesh beneath the rod; –

Death multitudinous as their frustrate spore! –
This has been done to us, Lord, thought-lost God;
And things still hidden, and unspeakable more.
   A world is emptied. Marked is that world's map
The forest color. There where thy people praised
In angular ecstasy thy name, thy Torah
Is less than a whisper of its thunderclap.
Thy synagogues, rubble. Thy academies,
Bright once with talmud brow and musical
With song alternative in exegesis,
Are silent, dark. They are laid waste, thy cities,
Once festive with thy fruit-full calendar,
And where thy curled and caftan'd congregations
Danced to the first days and the second star,
Or made the marketplaces loud and green
To welcome in the Sabbath Queen;
Or through the nights sat sweet polemical
With Rav and Shmuail (also of the slain), –
O there where dwelt the thirty-six, – world's pillars! –
And tenfold Egypt's generation, there
Is nothing, nothing ... only the million echoes
Calling thy name still trembling on the air.

Look down, O Lord, from thy abstracted throne!
Look down! Find out this Sodom to the sky
Rearing and solid on a world atilt
The architecture by its pillars known.
This circle breathed hundreds; that round, thousands, –
And from among the lesser domes descry
The style renascent of Gomorrah built.
See where the pyramids
Preserve our ache between their angled tons:
Pass over, they have been excelled. Look down
On the Greek marble that our torture spurned –
The white forgivable stone.
The arch and triumph of subjection, pass;
The victor, too, has passed; and all these spires
At whose foundations, dungeoned, the screw turned

Inquisitorial, now overlook –
They were delirium and sick desires.
But do not overlook, O pass not over
The hollow monoliths. The vengeful eye
Fix on these pylons of the sinister sigh,
The well-kept chimneys daring towards the sky!
From them, now innocent, no fumes do rise.
They yawn to heaven. It is their ennui:
Too much the slabs and ovens, and too many
The manshaped loaves of sacrifice!
   As thou didst do to Sodom, do to them!
But not, O Lord, in one destruction. Slow,
Fever by fever, limb by withering limb,
Destroy! Send through the marrow of their bones
The pale treponeme burrowing. Let there grow
Over their eyes a film that they may see
Always a carbon sky! Feed them on ash!
Condemn them double deuteronomy!
All in one day pustule their speech with groans,
Their bodies with the scripture of a rash,
With boils and buboes their suddenly-breaking flesh!
When their dams litter, monsters be their whelp,
Unviable! Themselves, may each one dread,
The touch of his fellow, and the infected help
Of the robed fauna with their tubes and shears!
Fill up their days with funerals and fears!
Let madness shake them, – rooted down – like kelp.
And as their land is emptying, and instructed,
The nations cordon the huge lazaret, –
The paring of thy little fingernail
Drop down: the just circuitings of flame,
And as Gomorrah's name, be their cursed name!

Not for the judgment sole, but for a sign
Effect, O Lord, example and decree,
A sign, the final shade and witness joined
To the shadowy witnesses who once made free
With that elected folk thou didst call thine.

Before my mind, still unconsoled, there pass
The pharaohs risen from the Red Sea sedge,
Profiled; in alien blood and peonage
Hidalgos lost; shadows of Shushan; and
The Assyrian uncurling into sand; –
Most untriumphant frieze! and darkly pass
The shades Seleucid; dark against blank white
The bearded ikon-bearing royalties –
All who did waste us, insubstantial now,
A motion of the mind. O unto these
Let there be added, soon, as on a screen,
The shadowy houndface, barking, never heard,
But for all time a lore and lesson, seen,
And heeded; and thence, of thy will our peace.
    Vengeance is thine, O Lord, and unto us
In a world, wandering, amidst raised spears
Between wild waters, and against barred doors,
There are no weapons left. Where now but force
Prevails, and over the once-blest lagoons
Mushroom new Sinais, sole defensive is
The face turned east, and the uncompassed prayer.
Not prayer for the murdered myriads who
Themselves white liturgy before thy Throne
Are of my prayer; but for the scattered bone
Stirring in Europe's camps, next kin of death,
My supplication climbs the carboniferous air.
Grant them Ezekiel's prophesying breath!
Isaiah's cry of solacing allow!
O thou who from Mizraim once didst draw
Us free, and from the Babylonian lair;
From bondages, plots, ruins imminent
Preserving, didst keep Covenant and Law,
Creator, King whose banishments are not
Forever, – for thy Law and Covenant,
O for thy promise and thy pity, now
At last this people to its lowest brought
Preserve! Only in thee our faith. The word
Of eagle-quartering kings ever intends

Their own bright eyrie; rote of parakeet
The laboring noise among the fabians heard;
Thou only art responseful.
                                    Hear me, who stand
Circled and winged in vortex of my kin:
Forego the complete doom! The winnowed, spare!
Annul the scattering, and end! And end
Our habitats on water and on air!
Gather the flames up to light orient
Over the land; and that funest eclipse,
Diaspora-dark, revolve from off our ways!
Towered Jerusalem and Jacob's tent
Set up again; again renew our days
As when near Carmel's mount we harbored ships,
And went and came, and knew our home; and song
From all the vineyards raised its sweet degrees,
And thou didst visit us, didst shield from wrong,
And all our sorrows salve with prophecies;
    Again renew them as they were of old,
    And for all time cancel that ashen orbit
    In which our days, and hopes, and kin, are rolled.

Who Hast Fashioned

Blessed art thou, O Lord,
    Who in Thy wisdom has fashioned man as Thou hast
fashioned him: hollowed and antrious, grottoed and gutted,
channelled; for mercy's sake gifted with orifice, exit, and vent!
    Did one of these only suffer obstruction, survives not the
hour that man!
    Thy will according, there drops the baneful excess: the scruff
falls; from the pores surreptitious the sweat; and the nails of the
fingers are cut; the demons are houseless.

Be blessed for the judgment of the eight great gates who dost diminish us to make us whole; for the piecemeal deaths that save; for wax and cerumen, which preserve all music, and for flux of the sinus, which gives the brain coolness, its space, and for spittle prized above the condiments of Asia; even for tears.

Benedictions

For that he gave to a stone understanding to understand direction.
For that he made no slave for me.
For that he clothes the naked with the nudities of beasts.
For that he erects the contracted.
For that he smites me each dawn with a planet.

Stance of the Amidah

O Lord, open thou my lips; and my mouth shall declare thy praise:

God of Abraham, God of Isaac, God of Jacob, who hast bound to the patriarchs their posterity and hast made thyself manifest in the longings of men and hast condescended to bestow upon history a shadow of the shadows of thy radiance;

Who with the single word hast made the world, hanging before us the heavens like an unrolled scroll, and the earth old manuscript, and the murmurous sea, each, all-allusive to thy glory, so that from them we might conjecture and surmise and almost know thee;

Whom only angels know
Who in thy burning courts
Cry: Holy! Holy! Holy!
While mortal voice below
With seraphim consorts
To murmur: Holy! Holy!
Yet holiness not know.

Favour us, O Lord, with understanding, who hast given to the bee its knowledge and to the ant its foresight, to the sleeping bear Joseph's prudence, and even to the dead lodestone its instinct for the star, favour us with understanding of what in the inscrutable design is for our doomsday-good;

O give us such understanding as makes superfluous second thought; and at thy least, give us to understand to repent.

At the beginning of our days thou dost give – O! at the end, forgive!

Deem our affliction worthy of thy care, and now with a last redeeming, Redeemer of Israel, redeem!

Over our fevers pass the wind of thy hand; against our chills, thy warmth. O great Physician, heal us! and shall we ailing be healed.

From want deliver us. Yield the earth fruitful. Let rain a delicate stalk, let dew in the bright seed, sprout ever abundance. Shelter us behind the four walls of thy seasons, roof us with justice, O Lord, who settest the sun to labour for our evening dish!

Thyself do utter the Shma! Sound the great horn of our freedom, raise up the ensign of freedom, and gather from the four corners of the earth, as we do gather the four fringes to kiss them, thy people, thy folk, rejected thine elect.

Restore our judges as in former times restore our Judge. Blessed art thou, O Lord, King, who lovest righteousness and judgement.

Favour them, O Lord, thy saints thy paupers, who do forgo all other thy benedictions for the benediction of thy name.

O build Jerusalem!

Anoint thy people David!

Our prayers accept, but judge us not through our prayers: grant them with mercy.

Make us of thy love a sanctuary, an altar where the heart may cease from fear, and evil a burnt offering is consumed away, and good, like the fine dust of spices, an adulation of incense, rises up.

O accept, accept, accept our thanks for the day's three miracles, of dusk, of dawn, of noon, and of the years which with thy presence are made felicitous.

Grant us – our last petition – peace, thine especial blessing, which is of thy grace and of the shining and the turning of thy Face.

Of the Making of Gragers

The following are the proper instruments wherewith Haman and all of that ilk may best be confounded:

clappers	utterants	&	mutterants
racketrakers	funaphores		hullabellows
filippics	titus-taps		sonorosnorers
fracasators	clangabangs	&	clackacousticons
drums and bimbamboomicores			vociferators
nazinoisicans	palmapats		gourds
ratatats	cymbals	&	stridors
knuckleknacks & castanets			brekekex

ton' o' thunders   datadiscords
panpandemonia   torquemadatumps   borborigmi
brontobronks   chmelnizzicatos   pharophonics
hellodeons   whistles & fee-fi-fo-fifers
          etceterows

Spinoza: On Man, on the Rainbow

All flowers that in seven ways bright
Make gay the common earth,
All jewels that in their tunnelled night
Enkindle and flash forth

All these, now in the sky up-thrust,
To dazzle human sight
Do hang but on a speck of dust,
But dust suffused by light.

Translations of Bialik

O Thou Seer, Go Flee Thee – Away

'Fly! Run away!' Not such as I do run.
I followed cattle, they taught me to walk slow.
Slow comes my speech, my words come one by one
The strokes of an axe they come down, blow by blow.

The strokes fell false? ... Not mine, not mine the blunder.
Yours was the fault the strokes were falsely sunk:
My hammer struck, and found no anvil under;
My axe struck punk.

No matter; I accept my fate, retire,
And gird my gear about my loins once more:
A hired man, but cheated of his hire
I will return – at my pace – to my door;

And there, in the deep forest, will strike root
With the great sycamore, and there hold firm;
But unto you, – rot, fungus, trodden fruit –
I prophesy – the whirlwind and the storm!

A Spirit Passed before Me

A spirit passed before my face, it dazzled me; for an instant your fingertip, O Lord, quivered the strings of my heart.

I stood there humbled, hushed, all ardor quelled. My heart curled within me; my mouth could not muster a psalm.

And, in truth, with what was I to come into the Temple? And how could my prayer ever be pure?

For my speech, O Lord, is altogether abhorrent, has become a broth of abomination.

There is not a word in it that has not been infected to the root; not a phrase but heard and it is mocked, not a locution but it has boarded in a house of shame.

My doves, my pure doves, that I had sent forth at dawn towards the sky, at dusk they came back, and, behold, they were crows!

From their throats there issued the rook's cawing; their beaks stank of carcasses; naturalized of the dungheaps, my doves!

It encompasses me, this cluttering rampage of language, it surrounds me, like a wreathing of harlots gone out on the town.

They glitter their gewgaws and gauds, they preen themselves, their eyes are fucus'd red, rot is in their bones.

This is their grace.

And at their skirts there trail the imps of incest, bastards of the pen, the get of fancy, words monstrous, arrogant, loathsome, a flux from empty-cockled hearts.

As the wildgrass they grow, they multiply like the thistle, there is no escape from them.

Daily, as the gutters are swept and the urinals emptied, their fetor, too, rises and corrupts the air, penetrates even to the man shut solitary in his room, unsabbaths his peace.

Where shall I run from this stench? Where shall I hide from this jangle?
Where is the seraph and his gleed shall cauterize my lips?

Only in the twittering of the birds, twittering at sunrise, or in the company of little children, playing in the street their simple games, only there may I be cleansed.
I will go, therefore, I will mingle with them, I will join in the *aleph-bais* of their talk and their lessons: and in that clean breath feel clean again.

Stars Flicker and Fall in the Sky

Stars flicker and fall in the sky,
All melts in the gloom, part to part.
Darkness falls on the world, and falls
The shadow across my heart.

Dreams flicker and wane and fall;
Hearts blossom, and burst, and fade:
O, look in my heart and see
The ruin time has made!

All pray for the light, the light!
All pray for the rising sun.
But weary and dark are these prayers
Each ending as it was begun!

O, how the long nights drag on!
O even the moon cannot keep
Awake, but weary, must yawn,
Waiting for day and for sleep.

NOTES

SELECTED BIBLIOGRAPHY

INDEX OF TITLES

INDEX OF FIRST LINES

Notes

The textual and explanatory notes are based on the much fuller notes in the *Complete Poems*.

There is a brief textual note for each poem indicating the copy-text and the date of composition. When the date of composition cannot be assigned with certainty to a single year, the date is given as a range of years. Three kinds of ranges are represented in the *Selected Poems*:

1. 1945/1948   (*certainly* no earlier than 1945 and *certainly* no later than 1948)
2. c. 1945/c. 1948   (*probably* no earlier than 1945 and *probably* no later than 1948)
3. c. 1945/1948   (*probably* no earlier than 1945 and *certainly* no later than 1948)

Where necessary, explanatory notes are also provided immediately following the textual note. The function of these notes is to gloss obscure terms and references and to provide relevant information concerning Klein's life and times.

The following editions are cited in the notes: *The Prayer Book*, translated and arranged by Ben Zion Bokser, rev. ed. (New York: Hebrew Publishing Co. 1967); *The Riverside Shakespeare*, ed. G. Blakemore Evans et al. (Boston: Houghton Mifflin 1974); the Modern Library edition of *Ulysses* (New York: Random House 1934); the Knopf edition of *The Second Scroll* (New York: Alfred A. Knopf 1951).

The following abbreviations are used in the notes:

UNPUBLISHED WORKS BY KLEIN

MS   Manuscript in the A.M. Klein Papers, National Archives of Canada

SP   *Selected Poems* (1955) [MS 2041–116]

REFERENCE WORKS

JE   *The Jewish Encyclopedia.* New York and London: Funk and Wagnalls Co.
      1906 [passages marked by Klein in his copy are noted]
OED   *The Oxford English Dictionary.* Oxford: Oxford University Press 1928
S   Solomon Spiro. *Tapestry for Designs: Judaic Allusions in 'The Second
      Scroll' and 'The Collected Poems of A.M. Klein.'* Vancouver: University
      of British Columbia Press 1984

Comments by Klein cited as 'McGill Reading' are from a recording (in the
A.M. Klein Collection of the National Film, Television and Sound Archives) of
a reading given by Klein to the Canadian Authors' Association at McGill Uni-
versity, 22 November 1955. Written notes by Klein are identified as [K], and
their various sources are indicated at the appropriate points in the explanatory
notes.

PORTRAITS OF A MINYAN

Hath Not a Jew ... (1940), pp. 14–21; date of composition c. 1929/1929
Minyan: the quorum of ten adult Jewish males required for public worship
rashi script: The biblical commentary of Rashi (Rabbi Solomon bar Isaac) is
      traditionally printed in a small and quite distinctive script.
To Tau from Aleph: *Aleph* is the first letter of the Hebrew alphabet; *tau* is the
      Greek equivalent of *taf*, the last letter of the Hebrew alphabet.
Pintele Yid: (Yid.) 'Literally "little dot of a Jew," a metaphorical Yiddish
      expression for the modicum or ember of Jewishness that remains in every
      Jew despite outward assimilation' [S].
Kaddish: The mourner's *Kaddish* is a prayer recited by the nearest male kin,
      usually a son.
Reb: (Yid.) 'mister,' traditional title prefixed to a man's first name
milah-banquet: 'a feast accompanying the performance of ritual circumcision'
      [S]
The onion and the herring: 'traditional fare for the Saturday night meal called
      Melaveh Malkah, or "the ushering out of the Sabbath Queen"' [S]
On Ninth of Ab ... wailing beards: See note to *The burrs*, AUTOBIOGRAPHICAL
      [p. 172].
Purim ... Haman: See note to *the Haman rattle*, AUTOBIOGRAPHICAL
      [p. 172].
feasts of rejoicing ... the scrolls: Simhas Torah ('the rejoicing of the law'), a

celebration marking the conclusion of one annual reading of the Torah and the beginning of the next. It includes dancing with Torah scrolls around the synagogue.

Messiah's greeting ... roast leviathan: According to Jewish tradition, the coming of the Messiah will be celebrated by a feast of roast leviathan.

Shadchan: (Yid.) a matchmaker

caftan: common garb of east European Jews

pilpul: (Heb.) dialectical logic used in the study of Talmud

For in a single breath ... on the Persian gallows rose: 'According to tradition the reader of the Book of Esther at the Purim service ... must utter the names of the ten sons of Haman who were hanged ... in one breath to indicate they all mercifully died at once' [S].

But on the High, the Holy Days ... / While litanies are clamored: 'During the High Holy Days (New Year and Day of Atonement), it is customary to say the prayers louder than usual to prompt additional fervour' [S].

And the Man Moses Was Meek: 'Now the man Moses was very meek' [Numbers 12.3].

Homunculus ... four ells: Four ells, or cubits, is 'a standard talmudic measurement which defines the area of a person's immediate surroundings legally and symbolically' [S]. It is also the minimum area required for a grave.

OUT OF THE PULVER AND THE POLISHED LENS

Hath Not a Jew ... (1940), pp. 30–6; date of composition c. 1931/1931
   The Jewish philosopher Baruch (or Benedict) Spinoza (1632–77) was excommunicated by the Rabbinate of Amsterdam because of his pantheistic philosophy. The major source for the poem is *The Philosophy of Spinoza: Selected from His Chief Works*, with a life of Spinoza and an introduction by Joseph Ratner (New York: Modern Library 1927), of which Klein owned a copy. Unless otherwise noted, all quotations in the following notes are from Ratner.

Pulver: 'powder, dust' (OED)

Polished Lens: After his excommunication, Spinoza 'took up the trade of polishing lenses as a means of earning his simple bread' [p. xvii].

Baruch alias Benedict: Hebrew and Latin, respectively, for 'blessed': '... he changed his name from Baruch to Benedict, quite confident one can be as blessed in Latin as in Hebrew' [p. xvii; marginal marking].

ram's horn blown ... maledictory breath: '... Spinoza found himself cut off from the race of Israel with all the prescribed curses of excommunication upon his head' [p. xvi; marginal marking].

stiletto: '... an attempt had been made by one of the over-righteous upon Spinoza's life soon after he became an object of official displeasure' [pp. xvi–xvii].

Uriel da Costa: The 'indecisive martyr' [p. xii], Uriel da Costa (1585–1640), came from a family of Portuguese Marannos (Jews forced to practise their religion in secret) who had converted to Catholicism. He returned to Judaism and left Portugal for Amsterdam, where his unorthodox ideas angered the Jewish community. He was twice excommunicated, and he twice repented, but the humiliating penance he was forced to undergo the second time drove him to suicide.

threat ... bribe of florins: 'Report has it ... they offered Spinoza an annuity of 1,000 florins if he would, in all overt ways, speech and action, conform to the established opinions and customs of the Synagogue; or, if he did not see the wisdom and profit of compliance, they threatened to isolate him by excommunication' [p. xvi].

theorems ... two and two make four: 'Man, Spinoza held, is a part of Nature, and Nature is governed by eternal and immutable laws. It must be just as possible, therefore, to apply the mathematical method to man, as it is to apply it to matter' [p. xxviii; marginal marking].

the horrible atheist: '... a rumor spread that he had in press a book proving that God does not exist' [p. xix; marginal marking].

Cabbalist: a student of the Kabbalah, the central Jewish mystical tradition

Sanctum sanctorum: (Lat.) 'holy of holies'; the inner sanctuary of the Temple where the ark containing the tablets of Moses was kept

golden bowl of Koheleth: Koheleth is the Hebrew name for both the book of Ecclesiastes and its author, traditionally King Solomon. For the 'golden bowl' [Ecclesiastes 12.6] as the brain, see note to *the keepers of the house ... the strongmen ... the golden bowl*, A PRAYER OF ABRAHAM, AGAINST MADNESS [p. 168].

Shabbathai Zvi: Shabbathai Zvi (1626–76) proclaimed himself the Messiah and aroused enormous enthusiasm among his fellow Jews, especially those of eastern Europe. He went to Constantinople to convert the Sultan but was himself forced to convert to Islam under threat of death. Most of his followers despaired; some, known as the Sabbatians, continued to believe in him: '... many of the faithful were attracted by ... the strange hope of being saved from a bitter exile by a Messianic Sabbatai Zevi' [p. xii].

Took ... wife: Shabbathai Zvi performed a sacrilegious marriage ceremony between himself and the Torah, in fulfilment of a prophecy concerning the coming of the Messiah.

silken canopy: the *hupah* under which the Jewish wedding ceremony takes place

Thou art hallowed unto me: words spoken by the Jewish bridegroom to his
   bride as he places the ring on her finger
Mynheer: (Dutch) 'my lord'
consumptive: '... the fine dust he ground ... aggravated his inherited tuberculo-
   sis and undoubtedly considerably hastened his death' [pp. xvii–xviii; mar-
   ginal marking].

DESIGN FOR MEDIAEVAL TAPESTRY

Canadian Jewish Chronicle, 7 Nov. 1947, pp. 8–9; date of composition
c. 1931/1931
Reb: (Yid.) 'mister,' traditional title prefixed to a man's first name
Judengasse: (Ger.) ghetto, literally 'Street of the Jews'
yellow badge: In 1215 the Lateran Council decreed that Jews were required to
   wear an identifying badge, generally yellow.
Nahum-this-also-is-for-the-good: a reference to Nahum of Gimzo, a rabbi
   mentioned in the Talmud who always put the best interpretation on events
   by saying, *gam zu letovah*, 'this also is for the good.'
Epicure: The Hebrew word *apikoros*, meaning 'sceptic' or 'atheist,' derives
   from the name of the Greek philosopher Epicurus.
How long ... nod: 'How long wilt thou forget me, O Lord? for ever? how long
   wilt thou hide thy face from me?' [Psalms 13.1].
sable ... gules: black and red, in heraldry
Rashi ... Ibn Ezra ... / Maimonides: For Rashi see introductory note to A PSALM
   OF ABRAHAM, TO BE WRITTEN DOWN AND LEFT ON THE TOMB OF RASHI
   [p. 169]. Abraham Ibn Ezra (1089–1164) and Maimonides (Moses ben
   Maimon, 1135–1204) were leading philosophers and rabbinical commenta-
   tors.
Duns ... aquinatic Thomas: the scholastic philosophers, Duns Scotus and
   Thomas Aquinas
kiddush benediction ... wine: a prayer recited over a cup of wine to consecrate
   the Sabbath or a festival
eighteen prayers: the *shemoneh esreh* ('eighteen'), the main prayer at all ser-
   vices, also known as the *amidah*

HAGGADAH

Hath Not a Jew ... (1940), pp. 52–6; date of composition c. 1929/1929
   The *haggadah* is a book of readings for the *seder*, the evening meal on
the first and second nights of Passover.
dotted like th' unleavened bread: *Maẓah*, the unleavened bread which is eaten

during Passover, is punctured over all its surface before baking to help prevent it from rising.

The moon a golden platter: Passover begins at the full moon.

perruque: See note to *Wårsovian perruque*, AUTOBIOGRAPHICAL [p. 172].

Black Decalogue: As part of the Passover ritual, the ten plagues which God inflicted on the Egyptians [Exodus 7–12] are recited; as each plague is named, it is customary to dip one's finger into the wine and shake a drop onto one's plate.

Goshen: the area of Egypt where the Jews lived

The Bitter Dish: For the *seder* ritual a ceremonial plate is set out containing several symbolic foods. These include *mazah*, symbol of 'the poor bread which they ate in the land of Egypt'; *haroset* (a thick mixture of ground apples, walnuts, and cinnamon), symbol of the mortar used by the Israelites in building Egyptian cities; and *maror* (horseradish), symbol of the bitterness of slavery endured by the Israelites.

This is the bread of our affliction: the opening words of the prayer recited over the ceremonial plate

Song: In anticipation of the prophet Elijah, who will herald the coming of the Messiah, a special goblet of wine is filled and the door is left open.

Chad Gadyah: (Aramaic) 'one kid'; a song traditionally sung at the *seder*. This section is a free rendering of the song.

Shochet: (Heb.) ritual slaughterer

The Still Small Voice: 1 Kings 19.12

The heirloomed clock enumerates the tribes: a reference to the twelve tribes of Israel

Jerusalem, next year! Next year, Jerusalem: 'Next year in Jerusalem' is the closing chant of the *seder*.

PLUMAGED PROXY

Hath Not a Jew ... (1940), p. 60; date of composition c. 1928/1931

'"Plumaged Proxy" refers to the custom, still observed by orthodox Jews, which enjoins the pious to slay a rooster as proxy for the sinful soul before the Day of Atonement. The ritual killing of the fowl is preceded by the intonation of a prayer, while the rooster is circled over the head' [letter to *Poetry* magazine, 19 April 1931].

a beard / Pluck little feathers: 'The bearded ritual slaughterer *(shohet)* plucks little feathers from the neck of the fowl to prepare it for slaughter' [S].

a thumb / Press down your gullet: 'After drawing a sharp blade across the neck of a fowl to sever the trachea and esophagus, the ritual slaughterer presses his thumb upon the epiglottis to bare them. This assures him that they have indeed been severed' [S].

six score ... a ripe age: Jews traditionally specify a ripe old age as 120 years [see Genesis 6.3].

SCRIBE

Hath Not a Jew ... (1940), pp. 65–6; date of composition c. 1931/1931
Sheen of Shaddai: *Shin* is the first letter of *Shaddai*, one of the names of God. The leather thongs of the phylacteries are wrapped around the left arm and hand in such a way as to form the three-letter word *Shaddai* on the hand.
prayer-shawl ... pendules ... white and blue: The prayershawl is often blue and white and it has pendules or fringes *(zizit).*
Lilith: a female demon, symbol of lust and sexual temptation
imp alcoved in a finger nail: 'an allusion to the Jewish tradition that evil spirits are attached to the fingernails' [S]
three score years and ten: the traditional full measure of human life
that other ark: 'A coffin is called *aron* in Hebrew. The same word is used for the ark into which the Torah scroll is placed in the synagogue' [S].

A BENEDICTION

Poems (1944), p. 24; date of composition c. 1928/1931

WOULD THAT THREE CENTURIES PAST HAD SEEN US BORN

Hath Not a Jew ... (1940), p. 68; date of composition c. 1931/1931

THESE NORTHERN STARS ARE SCARABS IN MY EYES

Hath Not a Jew ... (1940), pp. 68–9; date of composition c. 1931/1931
the sweet-singer: King David, author of the Psalms
Mazel Tov: (Heb.; lit., 'good luck') congratulations

NOW WE WILL SUFFER LOSS OF MEMORY

Hath Not a Jew ... (1940), pp. 70–1; date of composition c. 1928/1931
ham ... milk ... fast-days: The offense of eating on fast-days is aggravated by the fact that meat is eaten with milk (the eating of meat and milk together being forbidden) and that the meat is pork, which is, in itself, not kosher.

SATURDAY NIGHT

Haboneh, Dec. 1931; date of composition c. 1931/1931
Main Street: St Lawrence Blvd, the old Jewish 'Main'
Eli, Eli, lama zabachthani: 'My God, my God, why hast thou forsaken me?';
the last words of Jesus on the cross [Matthew 27.46, Mark 15.34]. These
words are an Aramaic translation of Psalm 22.2. The original Hebrew ver-
sion in Psalm 22 formed the title of a popular Yiddish song.

DIALOGUE

Opinion 2, 12 (22 Aug. 1932), 12; date of composition c. 1930/1930
the golden land: a translation of the Yiddish phrase, *di goldeneh medinah*, a
common term for America
Ratno's muds: Klein was born in Ratno, in the province of Volhynia, in the
northwestern Ukraine.
Reb Yecheskel Chazan: *Reb* (Yid., 'mister') is a traditional title prefixed to a
man's first name; *Yecheskel* is Hebrew for Ezekiel; *chazan* is Hebrew for
cantor.
To doom Columbus: a reference to the proverbial Yiddish expression 'a curse
on Columbus'

MARKET SONG

Hath Not a Jew ... (1940), pp. 74–5; date of composition c. 1928/1931

HEIRLOOM

A.J.M. Smith, *The Book of Canadian Poetry* (1943), p. 397; date of composi-
tion c. 1932/1934
   Klein's own comments [K] are cited from a letter to A.J.M. Smith of 21
January 1943.
yahrzeit: (Yid.) 'Literally anniversary. It is customary to inscribe the date of
the passing of an ancestor on the fly-leaf of some sacred book. Special
prayers are said on that anniversary date' [K].
Baal Shem Tov: See note to *Baal Shem Tov*, AUTOBIOGRAPHICAL [p. 172].
no pictures: 'Hebrew prayer books are never illustrated. The only drawings
that appear in the liturgy are the signs of the Zodiac illustrating the prayers
for rain and fertility' [K].
midnight liturgy: In a note on this phrase from one of Klein's poetry readings
[MS 6036], Klein refers to *tikun lel shevuot*, the custom of staying awake on

the night of Shavuot to study Torah. The term 'midnight liturgy' usually refers to *tikun ḥazot*, prayers at midnight in memory of the destruction of the Temple and for the restoration of the Land of Israel.

BESTIARY

Carl F. Klinck and R.E. Watters, *Canadian Anthology* (1956), p. 382; date of composition c. 1932/1934

Bestiaries were medieval collections of fables about animals, intended as didactic religious and moral allegories. Klein's own comments [K] are cited from a letter to A.J.M. Smith of 21 January 1943.

The elusive unicorn: 'Canst thou bind the unicorn with his band in the furrow? or will he harrow the valleys after thee?' [Job 39.10; cited in K].

The golden mice, the five: After the Philistines captured the Holy Ark, they suffered a plague. They returned the Ark with an offering which included five golden mice [1 Samuel 6.4].

Gay peacock and glum ape: Klein's marginal notes to MS 2238 identify these as 'Solomon's peacock and ape' [1 Kings 10.22].

The fiery behemoth: Job 40.15–24

The crocodile's sneeze: the leviathan. See Job 41.18: 'By his neesings [i.e., sneezings] a light doth shine, and his eyes are like the eyelids of the morning.'

He sees ... sucking milk: 'The wolf also shall dwell with the lamb, and the leopard shall lie down with the kid ... and the lion shall eat straw like the ox' [Isaiah 11.6–7].

the roe and hind: See Song of Solomon 2.7, 3.5.

Bravely ... the basilisk: The basilisk, also known as the cockatrice, was a fabulous reptile, hatched by a serpent from a cock's egg. Its breath, and even its look, was fatal. The reference seems to be to Isaiah 11.8: 'and the weaned child shall put his hand on the cockatrice' den.'

Pygarg and cockatrice: 'Pygarg' is 'a kind of antelope – literally, the white-rumped animal' [K]. 'Pygarg' occurs in Deuteronomy 14.5 and 'cockatrice' in Isaiah 11.8 and 14.29.

the beast Nebuchadnezzar: 'This wicked King is reputed to have ended his days as a grass-eating animal' [K]. See Daniel 4.25–33.

BALLAD OF THE DANCING BEAR

Hath Not a Jew ... (1940), pp. 88–101; date of composition c. 1928/1931.
Correction: 'Orgres' (*Complete Poems*, line 119) to 'Ogres' (p. 38)
Pan: (Pol.) 'gentleman, lord, master'
chalos: (Yid.) special braided Sabbath breads

jargon: Yiddish

iotas of God's name: In prayerbooks, God's name, *adonai*, is represented by two *yods*; *yod* is the Hebrew equivalent of the Greek *iota*.

Flourishes on holy script: a reference to the *tagin* or 'crowns,' formed of three flourishes added by scribes to the tops of certain letters in the Torah

tfillin: (Heb.) phylacteries

Tzizith: (Heb.) fringes of the prayershawl

one / For whom God preserved the sun: a *lamed-vavnik*, one of the thirty-six (represented by the Hebrew letters *lamed* and *vav*) hidden saints on whom the existence of the universe depends

moujik: (Pol.) peasant

Zhid'l: (Pol.) contemptuous diminutive of *zhid*, Jew

BAAL SHEM TOV

Hath Not a Jew ... (1940), p. 108; date of composition c. 1934/1934
    The Baal Shem Tov (Israel ben Eliezer, c. 1700–60) was the founder of Chassidism. He was not a formal preacher but communicated directly with individuals, including women, children, and the common people. He was known for his love of nature and had a reputation as a miracle worker. See Klein's note to *Baal Shem Tov*, AUTOBIOGRAPHICAL [p. 172].

who bore children on his back to school: As a young man the Baal Shem Tov served as a teacher's assistant, whose job it was to bring children to school.

ELIJAH

Hath Not a Jew ... (1940), pp. 109–10; date of composition c. 1931/1931
    Elijah was a prophet in the Kingdom of Israel in the reign of Ahab and Ahaziah. Traditionally, he is the herald of the coming of the Messiah, and he is a favourite figure in Jewish folklore and legend.

Aleph ... Tauph: the first and last letters of the Hebrew alphabet

SCHOLAR

Hath Not a Jew ... (1940), pp. 112–13; date of composition c. 1933/1933

gemara ... mishna: The Talmud consists of the *mishna* and the commentary on it, the *gemara*; *gemara* is often used to refer to the Talmud as a whole.

small ... rashi script: The biblical commentary of Rashi (Rabbi Solomon bar Isaac) is traditionally printed in a small and quite distinctive script.

Babylon: Babylon was noted for its eminent academies.

THE VENERABLE BEE

Hath Not a Jew ... (1940), pp. 114–15; date of composition c. 1934/1934
Venerable Bee: a punning reference to the Venerable Bede, the eighth-century
  English theologian and historian
caftan: worn by east European Jews
besomim: (Heb.) spices used in the Havdalah ritual marking the end of Sab-
  bath
kiddush: The *kiddush* is recited over a cup of wine to consecrate the Sabbath or
  a festival.

REV OWL

Hath Not a Jew ... (1940), p. 115; date of composition c. 1932/1934
Rev: Yiddish for 'Rabbi'
shtreimel: (Yid.) a fur-trimmed hat, commonly worn by Chassidim on the
  Sabbath and festivals
tears gizzards ... *kosher*: Before an animal can be declared kosher, it must be
  checked to ensure that its entrails are normal.

ORDERS

Hath Not a Jew ... (1940), p. 116; date of composition c. 1926/c. 1928

DIARY OF ABRAHAM SEGAL, POET

Canadian Forum 12 (May 1932), 297–300; date of composition
c. 1932/1932
Abraham Segal: combines Klein's own first name and the last name of
  J.I. Segal, a prominent Montreal Jewish poet whose works Klein reviewed
  and translated
No cock rings matins of the dawn: 'Matins' is a traditional poeticism for
  morning bird song.
morn, in russet mantle clad: Hamlet 1.1.166
melodye / Maken the smalle fowles: 'And smale foweles maken melodye'
  [Chaucer, Prologue to the *Canterbury Tales*, 9].
The lark ... *arise*: 'Hark, hark, the lark at heaven's gate sings, / And Phoebus
  gins arise' [*Cymbeline* 2.3.20–1].
little birds make a sweet jargoning: 'Sometimes all little birds that are, / How
  they seemed to fill the sea and air / With their sweet jargoning!' [Coleridge,
  'Rime of the Ancient Mariner,' 360–2].

slug-a-bed: 'Get up, sweet slug-a-bed' [Herrick, 'Corinna's Going A-Maying,' 5].

braggadocio: 'empty vaunting' [*OED*]

ranunculi: (Lat.) 'little frogs'

cauchemars: (Fr.) 'nightmares'

worshippers before a mazda lamp: The mazda lamp was a widely used electric light bulb, named after the Persian god of light.

ye angels, weep: 'Tears such as Angels weep' [*Paradise Lost* 1.620]

What a piece of work ... the world: Hamlet 2.2.303–7

Dr. *Aesculapius Pavlov*: combining Aesculapius, the legendary Greek physician, and Ivan Petrovich Pavlov, the Russian physiologist and experimental psychologist

Blessed ... inherit the earth: 'Blessed are the meek: for they shall inherit the earth' [Matthew 5.5].

The Lord ... ends: Compare 'God moves in a mysterious way / His wonders to perform' [William Cowper, *Olney Hymns*, no. 35].

Open, ye gates ... door: 'Lift up your heads, O ye gates; and be ye lift up, ye everlasting doors' [Psalms 24.7].

Consider ... toil: 'Consider the lilies of the field, how they grow; they toil not, neither do they spin' [Matthew 6.28].

Moi ... doigts: (Fr.) 'As for me, I have Apollo at the tips of my ten fingers.'

de profundis: from the Vulgate translation of Psalm 130.1, 'Out of the depths have I cried unto thee, O Lord.'

Beneath ... Ophelia: This section, written in mock-Elizabethan English, contains numerous echoes of Shakespeare: 'fretted roof' [*Hamlet* 2.2.301]; 'swag-bellied' [*Othello* 2.3.78]; 'calibans' [Caliban in *The Tempest*]; 'immortal yearnings' ['immortal longings,' *Antony and Cleopatra* 5.2.281]; 'clink their canakins' [*Othello* 2.3.69–70]; 'brave oaths' [*As You Like It* 3.4.41]; 'fee-fi-fum' ['fie, foh, and fum,' *King Lear* 3.4.183]; 'flibbertigibbet' [*King Lear* 3.4.115]; 'bodkins' [*Hamlet* 3.1.75];'Let me lie in thy lap, Ophelia' [*Hamlet* 3.2.112]. The *OED* defines some of the more obscure Elizabethan terms as follows: 'byzant' (or 'bezant') – 'a gold coin first struck at Byzantium'; 'nockandro' – 'the breech'; 'brabble' – 'to quarrel noisily'; 'dudgeon' – 'a kind of wood used by turners, esp. for handles of knives, daggers, etc.'; 'placket' – 'an apron or petticoat.'

Herzl: Theodor Herzl, founder of modern Zionism

My idols ... shards: According to Talmudic tradition, Abraham shattered the idols belonging to his father, Terah.

La chair ... les livres: (Fr.) 'The flesh is sad, alas, and I have read all the books'; the first line of Mallarmé's sonnet 'Brise marine'

macaronics: Macaronic verse was originally a burlesque form in which vernacular words are given Latin endings and used in Latin constructions. The word eventually came to designate any verse in which there is a mixture of languages, or, more broadly, any jumble or medley.

FROM 'OF CASTLES IN SPAIN'

Canadian Forum 18 (June 1938), 79; date of composition c. 1938/1938

FROM 'BARRICADE SMITH: HIS SPEECHES'

Canadian Forum 18 (Aug. 1938), 147–8 [sections I–II]; (Sept. 1938), 173 [section IV]; (Oct. 1938), 210 [section VI]; date of composition c. 1938/ 1938
sound / Of belching in the land: 'the voice of the turtle is heard in our land' [Song of Solomon 2.12].
create new heaven: 'For, behold, I create new heavens and a new earth' [Isaiah 65.17].
lotiferous: 'lotus-bearing'; not in the OED. In the *Odyssey* the lotus-eaters (*lotophagoi*) live in a state of dreamy forgetfulness induced by the fruit of the lotus.

IN RE SOLOMON WARSHAWER

A.J.M. Smith, *The Book of Canadian Poetry*, 3rd ed. (1957), pp. 352–6; date of composition c.1940/1940, revised c. 1953/1955
At his McGill reading of 22 November 1955, Klein made the following comments: 'There is a legend which says that when King Solomon had reigned upon his throne in ancient times for a number of decades, he was one day visited by the demon Asmodeus, with the cloven feet, the demon who knew how to break rocks, the demon who did not speak. The tale goes on to say that this Asmodeus flung King Solomon from his throne four hundred parasangs out of Jerusalem. And King Solomon thereafter went about in exile and everywhere announced that he was the king and nowhere was he believed, for Asmodeus sat upon the throne. And certainly during the short period when Hitler was enraged, rampant over Europe, it did seem as if Asmodeus was seated upon the throne of the world. For this legend for background, I imagine King Solomon persisting to the present day, and being that anonymous person who was captured by the Nazis in Warsaw in 1939. And it is concerning what took place then that this poem dedicates itself. It is a poem really about the nature of evil, the nature of the beast Asmodeus.'

Klein's further comments below [K] are cited from a letter to
A.J.M. Smith of 21 January 1943.

In Re: (Lat.) 'in the affair; in the matter of; concerning; regarding'

Vercingetorix: leader of the Gauls in a revolt against Rome; captured by Julius
Caesar and put to death. In 'The Book of the Year' [*Canadian Zionist* 3, 5
(Oct. 1936), 25], a review of *The Jews of Germany*, by Marvin Lowenthal,
Klein compares 'Vercingetorix, the old barbarian' and 'Hitler, the new one.'

nalewkas: 'Polish for "streets" – the slum district of Warsaw' [K]

The eldest elder of Zion: *The Protocols of the Elders of Zion* is a fraudulent
document reporting the alleged proceedings of a group of Jews in the nine-
teenth century planning world dominion. It was used by the Nazis, among
others, to justify anti-Semitism.

Ekaterinoslov: site of the execution of Tsar Nicholas II and his family by the
Bolsheviks

Mizraim: (Heb.) Egypt

lone star... Pharaoh's tomb: 'The architecture of the pyramids is such, that its
principal doorway or entrance is so placed, that the light of a star – name
forgotten – always falls upon it. cf. Hogben's Mathematics for the Million'
[K].

Ani Shlomo: (Heb.) 'The King in despair wandered over the countryside
crying "Ani-Shlomo – I am Solomon!" He was taken for a madman' [K].

did fling me from Jerusalem / Four hundred parasangs: 'Snatching up
Solomon, ... [Asmodeus] flung him four hundred parasangs away from
Jerusalem, and then palmed himself off as the king' [*JE*, 'Asmodeus'].

Beneath whose hem / The feet of the cock extend: In Jewish lore, demons have
the feet of cocks.

craved wisdom ... / The understanding heart: 'Give therefore thy servant
an understanding heart to judge thy people, that I may discern between
good and bad: for who is able to judge this thy so great a people' [1 Kings
3.9].

enthymemes: an enthymeme is 'a syllogism in which one premiss is sup-
pressed' [*OED*].

learned from beast ... bird: Solomon 'spake also of beasts, and of fowl, and of
creeping things, and of fishes' [1 Kings 4.33].

vanitatum vanitas: (Lat.) the Vulgate rendering of 'vanity of vanities,' a
phrase occurring in Ecclesiastes, traditionally ascribed to King Solomon

spread song: Solomon's 'songs were a thousand and five' [1 Kings 4.32].

that famous footstool for the Lord: the Temple. 'Thus saith the Lord,
The heaven is my throne, and the earth is my footstool: where is the house
that ye build unto me? and where is the place of my rest?' [Isaiah 66.1].

Qoheleth: Hebrew name for the Book of Ecclesiastes and its author

ten losing tribes: an allusion to the ten lost tribes, who constituted the northern kingdom of Israel, and who disappeared from history after being exiled by the Assyrians in 722 B.C.

Master of the worm, pernicious, that cleaves rocks: 'According to legend, Asmodeus was the master of the worm called Shani [*sic; should be* Shamir]. It could cleave rocks, and was very important in the construction of the Temple, since it was prohibited to put iron to Temple-stone. Hitler in his concentration camps is also such a master' [K].

lych-throne: 'corpse-throne'; not in the OED, but coined on analogy with 'lych-gate'

And further deponent saith not: a standard legal formula for concluding a deposition

A PSALM OF ABRAHAM, WHEN HE HEARKENED TO A VOICE, AND THERE WAS NONE

Poems (1944), p. 1; date of composition c. 1940/1941

Since prophecy has vanished out of Israel: 'alluding to the Jewish tradition that prophecy ceased in the fifth century B.C.E. with Hagai, Zechariah, and Malachi, the last of the prophets' [S]

Urim and Thummim: (Heb.) a priestly device for obtaining oracles, kept in the breastplate of the high priest [Exodus 28.30]

witch ... En-dor: After Samuel's death Israel was threatened by the Philistines. When God refused to answer King Saul's inquiries 'neither by dreams, nor by Urim, nor by prophets,' Saul had a witch at En-dor call up Samuel's spirit [1 Samuel 28].

scorpions ... whips: Rehoboam, the son of Solomon, said to the people of Israel when they complained of forced labour, 'My father hath chastised you with whips, but I will chastise you with scorpions' [1 Kings 12.11].

Baal: Canaanite fertility god, whose worship by the Israelites was frequently condemned by the prophets

A PSALM OF ABRAHAM WHEN HE WAS SORE PRESSED

Poems (1944), p. 4; date of composition c. 1940/1940

A PRAYER OF THE AFFLICTED, WHEN HE IS OVERWHELMED

Opinion 11, 12 (Oct. 1941), 28; date of composition c. 1940/1940

A PSALM OF ABRAHAM, CONCERNING THAT WHICH HE BEHELD
UPON THE HEAVENLY SCARP

Carl F. Klinck and R.E. Watters, *Canadian Anthology* (1955), p. 384; date of
composition c. 1941/1941
angels of Sodom: 'angels specially assigned to works of destruction, cf.
  Genesis, Chapter 19' [letter to A.J.M. Smith, 21 Jan. 1943]

GRACE BEFORE POISON

The Second Scroll (1951), pp. 190–1; date of composition c. 1940/1940

TO THE CHIEF MUSICIAN, WHO PLAYED FOR THE DANCERS

Poems (1944), p. 17; date of composition c. 1940/1940

A PRAYER OF ABRAHAM, AGAINST MADNESS

Poems (1944), pp. 27–8; date of composition c. 1940/1941
the keepers of the house ... the strongmen ... the golden bowl: 'In the day when
  the keepers of the house shall tremble, and the strong men shall bow them-
  selves ... or the golden bowl be broken' [Ecclesiastes 12.3, 6].
Behold him scrabbling on the door! / His spittle falls upon his beard: an allu-
  sion to the madness David feigned to escape Saul: 'And he changed his
  behaviour before them, and feigned himself mad in their hands, and scrab-
  bled on the doors of the gate, and let his spittle fall down upon his beard'
  [1 Samuel 21.13] .

A PSALM OF ABRAHAM OF THAT WHICH WAS VISITED UPON HIM

Canadian Jewish Chronicle, 21 Nov. 1952, p. 4; date of composition
c. 1940/1940

A PSALM TO TEACH HUMILITY

Poems (1944), p. 33; date of composition c. 1940/1940

A PSALM OR PRAYER – PRAYING HIS PORTION WITH BEASTS

Poems (1944), p. 34; date of composition c. 1941/1941
sheep ... sacrifice: Genesis 22.1–19

The dove ... / Sprigless: Genesis 8.8–9
The ass ... inspired minds: Numbers 22.28–30
David's lost and bleating lamb: 1 Samuel 17.34–5
Solomon's fleet lovely hinds: Song of Solomon 2.7, 3.5
food that desert ravens set: 1 Kings 17.6
the lion's honeyed fells: Judges 14.5–8
Azazel: On the Day of Atonement the high priest cast lots upon two goats, one 'for the Lord,' and the other 'for Azazel.' The former was slaughtered; the latter was sent out into the wilderness to 'make an atonement with God' [Leviticus 16.5–10]. The exact meaning of *Azazel* is unclear. Klein follows the King James version which translates it as 'scapegoat.'

A PSALM OF ABRAHAM, TO BE WRITTEN DOWN AND LEFT ON THE
TOMB OF RASHI

Canadian Jewish Chronicle, 10 April 1953, p. 10; date of composition
c. 1940/1940
    This psalm was occasioned by the nine-hundredth anniversary of the birth of Rashi (Rabbi Solomon bar Isaac), commentator on the Bible and the Talmud, born in Troyes in 1040; died there 13 July 1105. Rashi's commentaries are considered especially appropriate for students beginning their study of Scriptures.
images of god: 'So God created man in his own image, in the image of god created he him' [Genesis 1.27].
spiral splendid staircase: 'Nothing better describes the form of logic known as "pilpul" than to picture it as a "spiral splendid staircase" on which one rises ever upward, as in the Hegelian dialectic, upon the compatability of contradictions' [K; letter to Jewish Publication Society, 1 July 1943].
drink ... meat: Rashi 'seems to have depended for support chiefly on his vineyards and the manufacture of wine' [JE; marked].
Onkelus ... Jonathan: Onkelus and Jonathan ben Uzziel translated the Bible into Aramaic.
Yours were such days ... war: 'His last years were saddened by the massacres which took place at the outset of the first Crusade (1095–1096), in which he lost relatives and friends' [JE; marked].
Parshandatha of the law: Rashi 'won ... the epithet of "Parshandatha" (Esth. ix.7), taken by some writers as "parshan data" (= "interpreter of the Law")' [JE; marked].
left no son ... Kaddish: The mourner's *Kaddish* is a prayer recited by the nearest male kin, usually a son. Rashi left three daughters, but no son.

A PSALM TOUCHING GENEALOGY

Chicago Jewish Forum 3 (Spring 1945), 162; date of composition c. 1944/1944
They circle, as with Torahs: a reference to the *Simḥas Torah* celebration which
  includes dancing with the Torah scrolls around the synagogue

BALLAD OF THE DAYS OF THE MESSIAH

Poems (1944), pp. 61–2; date of composition c. 1941/1941
O Leviathan ... for the good: According to Jewish tradition, with the coming of
  the Messiah a banquet will be given by God to all the righteous, at which
  the flesh of the leviathan and the behemoth ('the wild ox') will be served.
piscedo: not in the OED; formed from *pisces,* Latin for 'fish'
pillared fire: 'And the Lord went before them ... by night in a pillar of fire, to
  give them light' [Exodus 13.21].

FROM *THE HITLERIAD*

The Hitleriad (1944); date of composition c. 1942/1943
Heil heavenly muse: 'Sing, Heav'nly Muse' [*Paradise Lost* 1.6].
hippocrene: a fountain sacred to the Muses. An allusion is probably intended
  to 'the true, the blushful Hippocrene' in Keats's 'Ode to a Nightingale,' 15.
lager: A pun may be intended on *Konzentrationslager*, 'concentration camp.'
Is this the face ... Rotterdam: 'Was this the face that launched a thousand
  ships, / And burnt the topless towers of Ilium?' [Christopher Marlowe, *The
  Tragical History of Doctor Faustus* 5.1.97–8, in *The Complete Plays*, ed. J.B.
  Steane (Harmondsworth: Penguin Books 1969), p. 330]. The entire centre of
  Rotterdam was destroyed by a German air bombardment on 14 May 1940,
  several hours after the city had capitulated.
vegetarian: Hitler was a vegetarian.
clown ... pranks: probably an allusion to Charlie Chaplin's satire on Hitler, *The
  Great Dictator*
the beast not blond: 'the magnificent blond beast, avidly rampant for spoil and
  victims' [Nietzsche, *Genealogy of Morals*, essay 1, aphorism 11]
His strength ... ten: 'My strength is as the strength of ten, / Because my heart
  is pure' [Tennyson, 'Sir Galahad,' 3–4].
Indited by his fellow-convict, Hess: Hitler dictated *Mein Kampf* to Rudolf
  Hess when they were in prison together after the 'beer hall *Putsch*.'
Junker: The Junkers were the Prussian land-owning class and main source of
  the Prussian officer corps. They were, on the whole, contemptuous of the
  Nazis but acquiesced in Nazi rule because of the privileges granted them.

Social Democrat; / *The Catholic, and concordat*: The Social Democrats were the most popular party in the Weimar Republic but were unable to come to terms with the Nazi threat. The Concordat of June 1933 gave the Catholic Church control over its own educational and communal institutions in return for recognition of the regime.

Thyssen, Hugenberg: Fritz Thyssen was the head of the German Steel Trust, which contributed substantial sums to the Nazis. Alfred Hugenberg was originally general manager of Krupps armaments; he served in Hitler's first cabinet.

umbrellas: Neville Chamberlain was often seen with an umbrella, most notably in a famous photograph taken on his return from signing the Munich Pact on 30 September 1938.

that voice ... brothers' blood: a reference to Cain's murder of Abel: 'the voice of thy brother's blood crieth unto me from the ground' [Genesis 4.10]

the lightning strokes the ten: the Ten Commandments, whose proclamation on Mount Sinai was accompanied by thunder and lightning [Exodus 19.16]

the bright freedoms four: the Four Freedoms proclaimed by Franklin Roosevelt on 6 January 1941 and incorporated into the Atlantic Charter (August 1941): freedom of speech and expression, freedom of worship, freedom from want, freedom from fear

AUTOBIOGRAPHICAL

The Second Scroll (1951), pp. 123–6; date of composition c. 1942/1942
        Klein's own comments [K] are cited from a letter to A.J.M. Smith of 21 January 1943.

Sabbath-goy: 'A Gentile employed by Jews to kindle their fires on the Sabbath, such labor being prohibited on that day to the children of Israel. Goy = Gentile' [K].

Torah-escorting band: 'The Torah is the scroll of the Law, written on parchment. When such a scroll is donated to a synagogue by a rich knave who seeks with his piety to atone for the wretchedness of his soul, the said scroll is customarily carried from the home of the donor through the streets leading to the synagogue, the whole to the accompaniment of music, to wit, a couple of violins and a flute' [K].

Ashkenazi: a common Jewish surname. Ashkenazi (Heb., 'German') Jews are of central European descent, as opposed to Sephardi (Heb., 'Spanish') Jews who are descended from the Jews of Spain and Portugal.

Maariv: 'The evening prayer. I will not say "vespers" ' [K].

Volhynia: a province in the northwest Ukraine 'formerly belonging to Russia, subsequently to Poland, and now in German hands' [K]

the four-legged aleph: 'The first letter of the Hebrew alphabet. cf. Alpha. Called "running" because written א with four legs, like a swastika' [K].

angel pennies: 'If I knew my lesson well, my father would, unseen, drop a penny on my book, and then proclaim it the reward of angels for good study' [K].

Warsovian perruque: 'Jewesses (married and pious) wear perruques. The custom has died out in America; but not for my mother.'

Baal Shem Tov: 'Literally, the Master of the Good Name – a saintly rabbi of the eighteenth century, founder of the movement known as Chassidism; he placed good works above scholarship. He was a simple good man, a St. Francis of Assisi, without birds or flowers' [K].

Hazelnut games: Games with hazelnuts were traditionally played by children during Passover.

The burrs: 'The Ninth of Ab (a month of the Jewish calendar) commemorates the destruction of the Temple. It is a day of mourning and fasting. It is customary on that day for youngsters to gather burrs and thistles, bring them to the synagogue, and throw them – not always with impunity – into the beards of the mourning elders – so as to give a touch of realism to their historic weeping. For the kids, this is a lot of fun' [K].

the Haman rattle: 'Haman is the villain of the Book of Esther. On Purim, which is the festival commemorating its events, the Book of Esther is read in the synagogue. Every time the name of Haman is uttered by the reader of the scroll, the youngsters, armed with rattles, make a furious noise, so as to drown out those unspeakable syllables. There will be a day when they will be called Hitler-rattles!' [K].

The Torah-dance on Simchas-Torah night: *Simḥas Torah* (lit. 'the rejoicing of the law') is a celebration marking the conclusion of one annual reading of the Torah and the beginning of the next. It includes dancing with Torah scrolls around the synagogue.

MONTREAL

The Rocking Chair and Other Poems (1948), pp. 29–31; date of composition c. 1944/1944

The poem is preceded by the following note in *Preview* 21 (Sept. 1944), 3–5, signed A.M.K.: 'Suiting language to theme, the following verse, – as will be noted, is written in a vocabulary which is not exactly orthodox English. It is written so that any Englishman who knows no French, and any Frenchman who knows no English (save prepositions – the pantomime of inflection) can read it intelligently. It contains not a word, substantive, adjectival, or operative, which is not either similar to, derivative from, or akin to a French word of like import; in short, a bilingual poem.'

sainted routs: Many of Montreal's streets are named after saints. St Lawrence Boulevard, 'the Main,' was the centre of the Jewish district, and for many years Klein lived on St Urbain Street. He had law offices on Ste Catherine Street and St James Street.

erablic: from *érable*, 'maple'

pendent balcon and escalier'd march: Montreal row-housing architecture, common on the streets of Klein's youth, is characterized by balconies and by iron staircases descending from the second storey.

Ville-Marie: the mission settlement, founded 1642, out of which Montreal grew

calumet / ... peace: ritual pipe used by Plains Indians

His statue in the square: The statue of Maisonneuve in Place d'Armes has four figures at its base, including an Iroquois.

Ecossic: from *écossais*, 'Scottish'

Hochelaga: the Indian village on whose site Montreal was founded

hebdomad: 'week.' Compare the French adjective *hebdomadaire*.

LES VESPASIENNES

A.M. Klein Papers, SP 2107–8; date of composition c. 1942/1944

Vespasiennes are public urinals, named after the Emperor Vespasian, who was the first to establish them in Rome. Vespasian was emperor at the time of the destruction of the second Temple, in A.D. 70.

DENTIST

Preview 20 (May 1944), 12; date of composition c. 1942/1942

BASIC ENGLISH

Canadian Forum 24 (Sept. 1944), 138; date of composition c. 1944/1944

In his McGill reading of 22 November 1955, Klein said of BASIC ENGLISH that it was written 'at a time when I was disappointed to learn that the great Sir Winston Churchill had endorsed Basic English as a medium of communication. I felt that Basic English, a vocabulary limited to 800 words, while good enough for the purposes of urgent and emergency communication, hardly constituted a language upon which one could build a literature. And therefore ... I submitted with respect to Sir Winston my comments touching Basic English of Mr I.A. Richards.'

grunt of Caliban: Before being taught language by Prospero and Miranda, Caliban 'would ... gabble like / A thing most brutish' [*The Tempest* 1.2.356–7].

Exhausted well of English, and defiled: Edmund Spenser refers to Chaucer as a 'well of English undefiled' [*The Faerie Queene* 4.2.32.8].

desesperanto: a pun on *désespoir* and Esperanto

BREAD

The Rocking Chair and Other Poems (1948), p. 14; date of composition c. 1944/1944

Bakers most priestly ... / White Levites: One of the priestly tasks of the Levites was to bake bread used in sacrificial offerings [Leviticus 2].

AND IN THAT DROWNING INSTANT

The Second Scroll (1951), pp. 195–7; date of composition c. 1943/1943

Basle print: The reference is unclear. Klein may be referring to the fact that Basle, Switzerland, was an important centre for the printing of Hebrew books at the end of the sixteenth century. There may also be a reference to Basle's historical significance as the site of the first international Zionist convention.

Baal Shem Tov: See Klein's note on *Baal Shem Tov*, AUTOBIOGRAPHICAL [p. 172].

Amsterdam: Amsterdam was an important centre of Jewish culture in the seventeenth century.

Abraham: Abraham Athias was put to death by the Inquisition in Cordoba in 1665.

arch: the Arch of Titus, commemorating Titus's victory over the Jews and his destruction of the second Temple

SONNET UNRHYMED

Accent 5, 4 (Summer 1945), 197; date of composition c. 1945/1945

Abba: The word *abba* is Hebrew for father; *abba* is also the rhyme scheme of the first quatrain of a Petrarchan sonnet.

the entangled branches ... Absaloms: Absalom was the third son of King David. He rebelled against his father and was defeated. When he was trying to escape, his long hair became entangled in the branches of a tree and he was killed by one of David's followers [2 Samuel 18.9–17].

PORTRAIT OF THE POET AS LANDSCAPE

The Rocking Chair and Other Poems (1948), pp. 50–6; date of composition
c. 1944/1945. Correction: 'trick' (*Complete Poems*, line 150) to 'trick,' (p. 104)
    PORTRAIT was reprinted in *Longer Poems for Upper-School, 1955–1956,*
ed. Roy Allin and Alan F. Meikeljohn (Toronto: Ryerson Press 1955). Some of
the notes for this edition were provided by Klein himself. These [K] are cited
below.
bereaved with bartlett: 'Since the editorial writer feels no real sense of loss, he
    resorts to quotes from Bartlett's *Familiar Quotations*. These quotes are so
    impersonal that bartlett becomes a common noun' [K].
Lycidas: Milton's pastoral elegy 'Lycidas' is a lament for the poet Edward
    King, who drowned at an early age. Through the figure of the shepherd
    Lycidas, Milton explores the nature of the poetic vocation.
the seven-circled air: 'A reference to Dante's *Inferno*. In Hell, various actions
    were punished in different circles, the total being seven according to Aristo-
    tle' [K]. The total in Dante's *Inferno* is actually nine.
quintuplet senses: 'This refers to a modern theory that each sense is a dupli-
    cate of the other; thus a situation may be "seen" through the sense of taste
    and "felt" through the sense of sight. Quintuplet also has a special signifi-
    cance in Canada' [K]. 'Special significance in Canada' is a reference to the
    Dionne quintuplets, born on 24 May 1934 in Corbeil, Ontario.
patagonian in their own esteem: 'The patagonians were a mythical tribe of
    giants. Seventeenth century travellers claimed to have seen them in South
    America. Thus some poets, having joined a party, believe themselves to be
    worldshakers' [K].
ape mimesis: 'The mimicry or imitation practiced by the ape. The poet's moti-
    vation is not merely the desire to imitate his predecessors' [K].
merkin joy: 'The mere joy of self-satisfaction' [K]. A merkin is 'counterfeit
    hair for women's privy parts' [OED].
the nth Adam ... naming: 'whatsoever Adam called every living creature, that
    was the name thereof' [Genesis 2.19].

THE ROCKING CHAIR

The Rocking Chair and Other Poems (1948), p. 1; date of composition
c. 1945/1945
St. Malo: the birthplace of Jacques Cartier
like some Anjou ballad: The French region of Anjou has no very close connec-
    tion with either ballads or Quebec. Klein may intend a pun on the syllable
    'jou' and 'Jew.'

THE PROVINCES

The Rocking Chair and Other Poems (1948), pp. 2–3; date of composition c. 1945/1945

the two older ones: Ontario and Quebec

their fathers: England and France

the three flat-faced blond-haired husky ones: the Prairie provinces: Manitoba, Saskatchewan, and Alberta

the little girl: Prince Edward Island. A reference may be intended to Prince Edward Island's most famous literary heroine, Anne of Green Gables.

her brothers: Nova Scotia and New Brunswick

the hunchback: British Columbia, a hunchback because of the Rocky Mountains which form its spine

Nine of them: At the time the poem was written, there were only nine Canadian provinces, Newfoundland not becoming the tenth until 1949.

the adopted boy of the golden complex ... / the proud collateral albino: the two Territories: the Yukon, site of the Klondike gold rush, and the Northwest Territories

the house with towers ... carillon of laws: the parliamentary buildings in Ottawa, dominated by the Peace Tower, which houses a carillon

THE CRIPPLES

The Rocking Chair and Other Poems (1948), p. 4; date of composition c. 1945/1946

Oratoire de St. Joseph: St Joseph's Oratory, a massive domed structure, was constructed on the site of a small chapel built by Brother André (Alfred Bessette, 1845–1937), a porter at Notre Dame College, who became known for his piety and healing powers. The Oratory is a centre for pilgrims, especially those seeking miracle cures, many of whom climb the stairs leading up to it on their knees.

heads, upon the ninetynine trays: a reference to John the Baptist, whose head was presented 'in a charger' to the niece of Herod, after he was beheaded at her request [Matthew 14]

ransomed crutches: Crutches abandoned by the miraculously healed are displayed in great numbers at the Oratory.

sanatorial: not in the OED; perhaps a combination of 'sanatory' (i.e., 'healing') and 'janitorial,' with reference to Brother André's role as porter

God mindful of the sparrows: 'Are not two sparrows sold for a farthing? and one of them shall not fall on the ground without your Father' [Matthew 10.29].

THE SNOWSHOERS

The Rocking Chair and Other Poems (1948), p. 5; date of composition
c. 1945/1946
goodlucks: The prints of the snowshoes in the snow presumably remind Klein
  of horseshoes, symbols of good luck. There may also be an allusion to *mazel
  tov*, the Hebrew expression for 'congratulations,' meaning, literally, 'good
  luck.'

FOR THE SISTERS OF THE HOTEL DIEU

The Rocking Chair and Other Poems (1948), p. 6; date of composition
c. 1945/1946
      '[W]hen I fell ill as a child [Klein broke his leg in a skating accident] ... I
was taken and nursed back to health by the sisters of the Hôtel Dieu. And it is
to thank them that I have penned these few lines' [McGill reading, 22 Nov.
1955].

GRAIN ELEVATOR

The Rocking Chair and Other Poems (1948), p. 7; date of composition
c. 1945/1946
      The reference is to the large concrete grain elevators in Montreal har-
bour.
babylonian: the Tower of Babel [Genesis 11.1–9]
Leviathan: Job 41
ark: Noah's ark [Genesis 6–9]
Josephdream: 'And [Joseph] said unto [his brothers], Hear, I pray you, this
  dream which I have dreamed: For, behold, we were binding sheaves in the
  field, and, lo, my sheaf arose, and also stood upright; and, behold, your
  sheaves stood round about, and made obeisance to my sheaf' [Genesis
  37.6–7].
scruples of the sun: A scruple is 'a small unit of weight or measurement'
  [*OED*].

UNIVERSITÉ DE MONTRÉAL

The Rocking Chair and Other Poems (1948), pp. 8–9; date of composition
c. 1947/1947

Klein graduated in law from the Faculté de Droit of the Université de Montréal.

Code Napoléon: (Fr.) the name given in 1807 to the French Civil Code. Since 1870 it has been referred to in France as simply the Civil Code, but it continues to be known as the *Code Napoléon* in Quebec to distinguish it from the Quebec Civil Code, which derives from it.

Place d'Armes: a square in old Montreal, site of the old Court House

the numbers and their truths: Articles in the Quebec Civil Code are numbered.

green raw ... warp and wrinkle into avocats: *Avocat* (Fr.) means both 'lawyer' and 'avocado.'

en bon père de famille: (Fr.) a phrase that occurs frequently in the Civil Code, indicating a standard of care that persons in certain positions (usually entrusted with the property of others) have to observe.

THE SUGARING

The Rocking Chair and Other Poems (1948), p. 10; date of composition c. 1945/1946

Maple trees are generally tapped around Easter, mid-March to mid-April; hence the Easter imagery of the poem.

Guy Sylvestre: Guy Sylvestre (b. 1918), critic, anthologist, and librarian, was an early admirer of Klein and encouraged interest in him in Quebec.

lenten ... ash: a reference to Ash Wednesday, which begins Lent

the honeyed dies / the sacred hearts, the crowns: In Quebec, maple sugar is traditionally prepared in moulds which sometimes take the shape of religious symbols.

INDIAN RESERVATION: CAUGHNAWAGA

The Rocking Chair and Other Poems (1948), pp. 11–12; date of composition c. 1945/1945

The Iroquois Indian Reserve of Caughnawaga is located on the south shore of the St Lawrence River, near Montreal.

alimentary shawls: In a letter, 12 July 1945, Marion Strobel of *Poetry* magazine inquired about the meaning of the phrase 'alimentary shawls.' Klein replied: 'The payment of the governmental allowance to Indian women upon reservations is made conditional on their wearing of the black shawl. Cf. the yellow badge – grassy ghetto indeed!'

KRIEGHOFF: CALLIGRAMMES

The Rocking Chair and Other Poems (1948), p. 13; date of composition
c. 1947/1947
Krieghoff: Cornelius Krieghoff (1812–72), painter of picturesque scenes of
   Quebec rural life
Calligrammes: title of a volume of poetry by Guillaume Apollinaire, in which
   the layout of the poems mimics their content

POLITICAL MEETING

The Rocking Chair and Other Poems (1948), pp. 15–16; date of composition
c. 1946/1946
      POLITICAL MEETING describes an anti-conscription rally addressed by the
mayor of Montreal, Camillien Houde.
the ritual bird ... alouette's: a paraphrase of the traditional French-Canadian
   song *Alouette*
the Grande Allée: (Fr.) the street in Quebec City where the most prominent
   Québécois lived; by extension, the élite of French Quebec

FRIGIDAIRE

The Rocking Chair and Other Poems (1948), p. 18; date of composition
c. 1945/1946
hill 70: a ski hill in the Laurentians. The context would seem to exclude an
   allusion to the more widely known 'Hill 70,' site of a major battle of World
   War I (15 Aug. 1917), involving Canadian troops.

DRESS MANUFACTURER: FISHERMAN

The Rocking Chair and Other Poems (1948), pp. 20–1; date of composition
c. 1947/1947
percer-proud: a pun on 'purse-proud' – 'proud of wealth; puffed up on account
   of one's wealth' [OED]. 'Percer' is an obsolete form of 'piercer' – 'an instru-
   ment or tool for piercing or boring holes' [OED]. Klein may intend a refer-
   ence to both a sewing needle and a fish hook.

THE BREAK-UP

The Rocking Chair and Other Poems (1948), p. 25; date of composition
c. 1945/1946

WINTER NIGHT: MOUNT ROYAL

The Rocking Chair and Other Poems (1948), p. 32; date of composition
c. 1947/1947

LOOKOUT: MOUNT ROYAL

The Rocking Chair and Other Poems (1948), pp. 33–4; date of composition
c. 1947/1947

THE MOUNTAIN

The Rocking Chair and Other Poems (1948), pp. 35–6; date of composition
c. 1947/1947
the famous cross: the electrically lit cross at the top of Mount Royal commem-
  orating Maisonneuve's vow to erect a cross on the mountain if he and his
  men survived their first winter in Montreal
pissabed dandelion, the coolie acorn: 'Pissabed' is a translation of the French
  word for dandelion, *pissenlit*. The acorn presumably suggests to the young
  Klein a head wearing a coolie hat.
Cartier's monument ... bronze tits of Justice: in Fletcher's Field, on the eastern
  slope of Mount Royal. It has various allegorical figures around its base,
  including a bare-breasted figure of Justice.

LONE BATHER

The Rocking Chair and Other Poems (1948), pp. 37–8; date of composition
c. 1947/1947

PASTORAL OF THE CITY STREETS

The Rocking Chair and Other Poems (1948), pp. 39–40; date of composition
c. 1947/1947
his ears, like pulpit-flowers: Jack-in-the-pulpit, a plant of the lily family, has a
  flower spike partly arched over by a hoodlike covering which resembles a
  horse's ear.

M. BERTRAND

The Rocking Chair and Other Poems (1948), p. 41; date of composition
c. 1945/1946

icitte: (Fr.) an archaic form of *ici* still current in Quebec popular speech
conférencier: (Fr.) lecturer

MONSIEUR GASTON

The Rocking Chair and Other Poems (1948), p. 43; date of composition
c. 1947/1947
vaurien: (Fr.) good-for-nothing

DOCTOR DRUMMOND

Canadian Forum 26 (Sept. 1946), 136; date of composition c. 1946/1946
William Henry Drummond (1854–1907) emigrated from Ireland to
Montreal as a child. He became a doctor and a poet, famous for his verse por-
traying French-Canadian *habitant* life in a dialect of his own devising.

PARADE OF ST. JEAN BAPTISTE

Huit poèmes canadiens (en anglais) (1948), pp. 14–16; date of composition
c. 1947/1947
On 24 June (St John the Baptist's day in the church calendar) the St Jean
Baptiste Society organizes activities, including parades, to celebrate Quebec's
national heritage. For the bilingual nature of the poem, see introductory note
to MONTREAL [p. 172].
enfilade: (Fr.) 'a group of objects placed one after the other'
ultramontane: Ultramontanism, the belief in the absolute supremacy of the
    Catholic Church in all aspects of society, was still a dominant force in Que-
    bec in Klein's day.
puissant: (Fr.) 'powerful'
crouped ... curvetting ... gambade: 'Croupade,' 'curvet,' and 'gambade' are all
    terms referring to 'a leap or bound of a horse' [OED].
Cendrillon: (Fr.) Cinderella
Massicotte: Edmond-Joseph Massicotte (1875–1929), Quebec artist and illus-
    trator, who depicted popular customs and traditions of Quebec
chasse-galerie: Quebec legend of hunters condemned to hunt throughout eter-
    nity in a canoe propelled through the air with the aid of the devil
Hébert: Louis Hébert, apothecary and colonist (1575–1627). He settled in
    Quebec in 1617, and his family was the first to cultivate land in Canada.
parish parallelograms: Under the seigneurial system, *seigneurs* were granted
    parcels of land which were divided into rectangular river-lots and leased to
    habitants.
gonfalons: (Fr.) 'banners'

catena: (Lat.) 'chain'

chrysostomate: This verb does not occur in the OED. The OED does have the adjectives 'chrysostomatical' and 'chrysostomic,' from the Greek for 'golden mouthed, an epithet applied to favourite orators.'

berceuses: (Fr.) 'lullabies.' There may also be an allusion to *la revanche des berceaux* ('the revenge of the cradles'), the high birthrate which helped to ensure the survival of 'philoprogenitive Quebec.'

blanched age: Klein may be using 'blanch' as a French form of 'blank,' in the sense of 'a vacant space, place, or period; a void' [OED].

infidelium partes: (Lat.) The term *episcopi in partibus infidelium* ('bishops in the territories of the infidels') is used of titular bishops whose dioceses are inaccessible because they are under non-Christian control.

Yamachiche: a Quebec village, whose old church is visited by many pilgrims

Ablute: derived from the past participle, *ablutus,* of the Latin *abluere*, 'to wash.' 'Ablute' is not in the OED, though 'abluted' is, an obsolete word meaning 'washed away, washed clean.'

the rotund mayor: Camillien Houde. See introductory note to POLITICAL MEETING [p. 179].

Cyrano: Houde had a very prominent nose, and as a young man he often played the title role of Rostand's *Cyrano de Bergerac* in amateur theatricals.

p'tit gars de Ste. Marie: (Fr.) Houde was first elected to publicoffice as the provincial member for the working-class riding of Ste Marie in east end Montreal. Throughout his life he continued to be known as the *petit gars de Ste Marie*.

annuair: from 'annuaire' (Fr.), 'year-book'

pères de famille: (Fr.) See note to *en bon père de famille*, UNIVERSITÉ DE MONTRÉAL [p. 178].

CANTABILE

Northern Review 2, 3 (Sept.–Oct. 1948), 30–1; date of composition 1948
CANTABILE is a parody/review of *The Cantos of Ezra Pound I–LXXX* (New Directions 1948)

De litteris ... ingeniis: (Lat.) 'about books, arms, and men of unusual genius' ['Canto XI']. Pound quotes Platina (Bartolomeo Sacchi, 1421–81), who was imprisoned for conspiracy against Pope Paul II.

il miglior fabbro: (Ital.) 'the better maker' [Dante, *Purgatorio* 26.117]

But bye ... St. Mary's Lough: the concluding stanza of the Scottish ballad 'The Douglas Tragedy.' The Douglas to whom Klein is alluding is Clifford Hugh Douglas (1879–1952), founder of the Social Credit movement, of which Pound was an adherent.

USURA: (Lat.) Pound saw usury as the root of all evil. See in particular the attack on 'USURA' in 'Canto XLV.'

χρύσω χρυσοτέρα: (Gr.) 'more golden than gold,' a fragment attributed to Sappho

bearded like the pard: Jacques's description of the *miles gloriosus* in his speech on the seven ages of man [*As You Like It* 2.7.150]

The art of conversation ... / small talk shouted: a paraphrase of Allen Tate's comment in his essay 'Ezra Pound': 'The secret of [Pound's] form is this: conversation. The *Cantos* are talk, talk, talk; ... they are just rambling talk' [*Collected Essays* (Denver: Alan Swallow 1959), p. 353].

traductore – tradittore: (Ital.) 'a translator is a traitor'

syphilisation: In the 'Cyclops' episode of *Ulysses*, the anti-Semitic 'citizen' responds to Leopold Bloom's defence of British civilization: 'Their syphilisation, you mean' [p. 319].

Rapallo: Pound lived in Rapallo, Italy, for many years.

Gradus ad parnassum: (Lat.) a Latin or Greek dictionary intended as an aid for students of Latin or Greek verse composition; the subtitle of Pound's *ABC of Reading*, of which Klein owned a copy

a compiler of several don'ts: an allusion to Pound's article 'A Few Don'ts by an Imagiste'

Jimmy ... poor Mr. Breen / ... E.P.: EP: 'Jimmy' is James Joyce. 'Poor Mr. Breen' is Dennis Breen, a pathetic lunatic mentioned in several chapters of *Ulysses*, including 'Cyclops' [p. 315], who is upset at receiving a postcard with the message 'U. p. up,' which he interprets as an attack on his virility. 'E.P.' is, of course, Ezra Pound, with specific reference to 'E.P. Ode pour L'Election de Son Sepulchre,' the first section of Pound's autobiographical *Hugh Selwyn Mauberley*.

'EP. Est Perditus: a reference to the medieval anti-Semitic taunt *HEP* (the apostrophe in *'EP* marking the elided *H*). It is sometimes explained as an acronym for *Hierosolyma est perdita* (Jerusalem is lost).

SESTINA ON THE DIALECTIC

A.M. Klein Papers, MS 2632-3; date of composition c. 1946/1946

'Dialectical thinking, the thinking of the dialectics of the Hegelian philosophy ... holds that all life is made up of thesis, antithesis, these resolving into a synthesis and this again breaking up into antithesis, and so the world moves like a pendulum, backward and forward and yet maintaining a kind of equilibrium as the pendulum reaches its central point. This pendulum effect is observable in many of the phenomena of nature, in the ebbing and flowing of human blood, in the ebb and flow of time, and appears also, according to

Hegel, to be a mode of general historical and human behaviour' [McGill reading, 22 Nov. 1955].

MEDITATION UPON SURVIVAL

Contemporary Verse 32 (Summer 1950), 9–10; date of composition
c. 1946/1946

ELEGY

The Second Scroll (1951), pp. 127–34; date of composition c. 1947/1947
the cubits of my ambience: See note to *Homunculus ... four ells*, PORTRAITS OF
  A MINYAN [p. 155].
iotas of God's name: See note to *iotas of God's name*, BALLAD OF THE DANCING
  BEAR [p. 162].
angular ecstasy: 'Jews, especially those of east European extraction, habitually
  sway back and forth from the hips during prayers, thus making "angles"
  with the rest of the body. This motion is traditionally considered an indica-
  tion of the worshipper's intense concentration' [S].
talmud ... song alternative in exegesis: The Talmud is often read in a singsong
  manner; its exegesis is 'alternative' since it proceeds dialectically.
curled and caftan'd: Curled earlocks (*peot*) and caftans were typical of the
  orthodox Jews of eastern Europe.
first days and the second star: 'The first days of biblical festivals are holy days
  ... and the appearance of the new moon, or "second star"... which begins a
  new lunar month, is also of special religious significance ... Both events are
  celebrated by special congregational prayers and ceremonies' [S].
To welcome in the Sabbath Queen: The Sabbath is traditionally personified as
  a queen or bride, and is welcomed as such by orthodox Jews at the beginning
  of each Sabbath.
Rav and Shmuail: two sages who laid the foundation of the Talmud. Their dis-
  cussions are frequently cited in the Talmud.
the thirty-six: the hidden saints on whom depends the existence of the uni-
  verse
tenfold Egypt's generation: Six hundred thousand Jews left in the exodus from
  Egypt [Exodus 12.37]; 'tenfold' six hundred thousand equals the six million
  Jews destroyed by the Nazis.
Look down ... Gomorrah: 'And the Lord said, Because the cry of Sodom and
  Gomorrah is great, and because their sin is very grievous; I will go down
  now, and see whether they have done altogether according to the cry of it,
  which is come unto me' [Genesis 18.20–1].

slabs ... ovens ... manshaped loaves of sacrifice: Klein links the ovens of the extermination camps, which had slabs for sliding bodies in, to the ritual bread baked by the Levites for use in the Temple sacrifices [Leviticus 2].

treponeme: the organism which causes syphilis

double deuteronomy: Deuteronomy 28.15–68 contains an extensive list of maledictions for those who disobey God.

The pharaohs ... royalties: This list of oppressors of the Jews who have passed into history include: Pharaonic Egypt; Spain, where Jews suffered expulsion or forced conversion in the fifteenth century; Persia (with its capital in Shushan), whose grand vizier, Haman, sought the total destruction of the Jews; Assyria, a powerful enemy of the ancient Israelites, responsible for the disappearance of the ten lost tribes; and the Seleucid dynasty, which, under King Antiochus IV Epiphanes, was defeated by the Maccabees.

of thy will our peace: 'E'n la sua volontade è nostra pace' [Dante, *Paradiso* 3.85]

Vengeance is thine: 'Vengeance is mine; I will repay, saith the Lord' [Romans 12.19].

The face turned east: Jews living west of Jerusalem face east when praying.

Ezekiel's prophesying breath: a reference to Ezekiel's vision of the resurrection of dry bones [Ezekiel 37.1–14]

Isaiah's cry of solacing: The later chapters of Isaiah, from chapter 40 on, contain messages of consolation for the exiled Jewish people.

Mizraim: (Heb.) Egypt

Babylonian lair: Spiro suggests two allusions: to Nebuchadnezzar's transformation to a grass-eating animal (see note to *the beast Nebuchadnezzar*, BESTIARY [p. 161]) and to the episode of Daniel in the lions' den [Daniel 6.16–23].

renew our days ... as they were of old: 'Turn thou us unto thee, O Lord, and we shall be turned; renew our days as of old' [Lamentations 5.21]. The verse is part of the Torah service on weekdays and the Sabbath.

Carmel's mount: a mountain range in northern Israel near the Mediterranean coast. Jeremiah 46.18 refers to 'Carmel by the sea.'

song ... raised its sweet degrees: Psalms 120–34 begin with the phrase 'A Song of degrees.'

WHO HAST FASHIONED

The Second Scroll (1951), pp. 189–90; date of composition c. 1950/1950

Like BENEDICTIONS and STANCE OF THE AMIDAH, WHO HAST FASHIONED is part of 'Gloss Hai' of *The Second Scroll*, which consists of 'drafts for a liturgy' [*The Second Scroll*, note, p. 119] attributed to Uncle Melech; it is an expansion of a benediction in the morning service: 'Praised be Thou, O Lord our God, King of the universe, who hast created man with wisdom and hast fashioned within him numerous orifices and passageways. It is well known, by the Law which Thou hast ordained, that if but one of these were impaired, we could not long continue to exist. Praised be Thou, O Lord, who art a wondrous healer of all Thy creatures.'

nails of the fingers ... demons: See note to *imp alcoved in a finger nail*, SCRIBE [p. 159].

eight great gates: 'the ears (2), nose (1), mouth (1), eyes (2), and lower orifices (2)' [S]

BENEDICTIONS

The Second Scroll (1948), p. 190; date of composition c. 1950/1950

BENEDICTIONS is based on five of the fifteen morning blessings, *birkot hashahar*. They all begin with the formula 'Praised be Thou, O Lord our God, King of the universe ...,' and the relevant ones continue: (1) 'who hast endowed the cock with the instinct to distinguish between day and night'; (2) 'who hast not made me a slave'; (3) 'who clothest the naked'; (4) 'who raisest up those who are bowed down'; and (5) 'who removest sleep from mine eyes and slumber from mine eyelids.'

STANCE OF THE AMIDAH

The Second Scroll (1948), pp. 193–5; date of composition c. 1950/1950

The *amidah*, or 'standing up,' is the core of every Jewish worship service. It is so called because the worshipper recites it while standing. It is also known as the *shemoneh esreh*, or 'eighteen,' because it originally consisted of eighteen benedictions. A nineteenth benediction, actually a curse directed at heretics, which was added at the time of the destruction of the second Temple, has no equivalent in STANCE OF THE AMIDAH.

The poem follows the structure of the *amidah* very closely. Like the *amidah*, it begins with Psalm 51.15 (italicized passage), and the eighteen verse paragraphs which follow correspond to the eighteen benedictions. In general, Klein elaborates more freely on the earlier benedictions than on the later ones, which are, for the most part, simply paraphrased or abridged.

hast made thyself manifest ... the shadows of thy radiance: no parallel in the *amidah*

Who with single word ... almost know thee: The corresponding benediction in the *amidah* has 'You are eternally mighty, O Lord, the Resurrector of the dead are you, abundantly able to save.'

Whom only angels know / ... not know: Like the corresponding benediction in the *amidah* (the 'sanctification'), this passage is ultimately based on Isaiah 6.3: 'And one cried unto another, and said, Holy, holy, holy, is the LORD of hosts: the whole earth is full of his glory.'

who hast given to the bee ... doomsday-good: no parallel in the *amidah*

such understanding: The corresponding benediction has 'Thy Torah.'

Shelter us behind ... evening dish: no parallel in the *amidah*

the Shma ... the four fringes to kiss them: The *shema* (so called from its opening words, *shema yisrael*, 'Hear, O Israel') is the central declaration of the Jewish faith. In the course of reciting the *shema* in the Morning Service, the worshipper gathers up the fringes on the four corners of the prayershawl and kisses them.

Make us of thy love a sanctuary ... incense, rises up: 'Show Thy favour, O Lord our God, unto Thy people Israel and heed their prayers; cause Thy service to be restored in Thy sanctuary in Zion, and mayest Thou receive therein with favour and with love their offerings and their supplications. And may the worship of Thy people Israel always be worthy of Thy acceptance.'

OF THE MAKING OF GRAGERS

Canadian Jewish Chronicle, 3 March 1950, p. 7; date of composition c. 1950/1950

See note to *the Haman rattle*, AUTOBIOGRAPHICAL [p. 172].

all of that ilk: includes notorious persecutors of the Jews throughout history: the Pharaohs ('pharophonics'); Titus, Roman general, later Emperor, who captured Jerusalem and destroyed the second Temple ('titus-taps'); Tomás de Torquemada, the first head of the Spanish Inquisition ('torquemada-tumps'); Bogdan Chmelnitzki, who led a revolt against Polish rule in the Ukraine in the seventeenth century which resulted in the death of many Jews ('chmelnizzicatos'); and Hitler ('nazinoisicans').

brekekex: (Gr.) an allusion to the refrain in the chorus of Aristophanes' *The Frogs, brekekekex-koax-koax*

borborigmi: from the Greek βορβορυγμός ('intestinal rumbling'). There is an entry in the OED under 'borborygm.'

SPINOZA: ON MAN, ON THE RAINBOW

A.M. Klein Papers, SP 2109; date of composition c. 1953/1955

For Spinoza, see notes to OUT OF THE PULVER AND THE POLISHED LENS [pp. 155–7].

TRANSLATIONS OF BIALIK

O THOU SEER, GO FLEE THEE – AWAY

A.M. Klein Papers, MS 5395; date of composition c. 1953/c. 1955
    The title is from Amos 7.12.

A SPIRIT PASSED BEFORE ME

A.M. Klein Papers, MS 5399–400; date of composition c. 1953/c. 1955

STARS FLICKER AND FALL IN THE SKY

A.M. Klein Papers, MS 5401; date of composition c. 1953/c. 1955

Selected Bibliography

WORKS BY KLEIN

The following volumes have so far appeared in the *Collected Works* being published by University of Toronto Press:

Beyond Sambation: Selected Essays and Editorials 1928–1955. Ed.
   M.W. Steinberg and Usher Caplan. Introd. M.W. Steinberg. 1982
The Short Stories of A.M. Klein. Ed. and introd. M.W. Steinberg. 1983
Literary Essays and Reviews. Ed. Usher Caplan and M.W. Steinberg. Introd.
   Usher Caplan. 1987
A.M. Klein: The Complete Poems. 2 vols. Ed. and introd. Zailig Pollock. 1990
Notebooks: Selections from the A.M. Klein Papers. Ed. Zailig Pollock and
   Usher Caplan. Introd. Zailig Pollock. 1994

Two further volumes in the *Collected Works* are currently being edited:
The Second Scroll, by Elizabeth Popham and Zailig Pollock; and the *Letters,* by
Elizabeth Popham and Harold Heft. Klein's novel, *The Second Scroll*, is
available in the New Canadian Library edition (McClelland and Stewart, 1994)
with an Afterword by Seymour Mayne.

BIBLIOGRAPHY

Zailig Pollock, Usher Caplan, and Linda Rozmovits. *A.M. Klein: An Annotated
   Bibliography.* Introd. Zailig Pollock. Toronto: ECW Press 1993

BIOGRAPHY

Usher Caplan. *Like One That Dreamed: A Portrait of A.M. Klein.* Toronto:
   McGraw-Hill Ryerson 1982

CRITICAL STUDIES

Miriam Waddington. *A.M. Klein.* Studies in Canadian Literature. Toronto: Copp Clark 1970

G.K. Fischer. *In Search of Jerusalem: Religion and Ethics in the Writings of A.M. Klein.* Montreal: McGill-Queen's University Press 1975

Solomon Spiro. *Tapestry for Designs: Judaic Allusions in 'The Second Scroll' and 'The Collected Poems of A.M. Klein.'* Vancouver: University of British Columbia Press 1984

Rachel Feldhay Brenner. *A.M. Klein, the Father of Canadian Jewish Literature: Essays in the Poetics of Humanistic Passion.* Lewiston,N.Y.: Edwin Mellen Press 1990

Noreen Golfman. *A.M. Klein and His Works.* Toronto: ECW Press [1991]

Zailig Pollock. *A.M. Klein: The Story of the Poet.* Toronto: University of Toronto Press 1994

COLLECTIONS OF ARTICLES

T.A. Marshall, ed. and introd. *A.M. Klein.* Critical Views on Canadian Writers, No. 4. Toronto: Ryerson 1970

Seymour Mayne, ed. and introd. *The A.M. Klein Symposium.* Reappraisals: Canadian Writers, No. 2. Ottawa: University of Ottawa Press 1975

Zailig Pollock, ed. and introd. *Journal of Canadian Studies / Revue d'études canadiennes* [A.M. Klein's Montreal / A.M. Klein à Montréal] (Summer 1984)

Index of Titles

Index of First Lines